BRUM'S ... WORD

Malcolm Boyden

The Parrs Wood Press
MANCHESTER

First Published 2003

THE PARRS WOOD PRESS
St Wilfrid's Enterprise Centre
Royce Road, Manchester, M15 5BJ
www.parrswoodpress.com

© Malcolm Boyden 2003

ISBN: 1 903158 50 8

Printed by Newton Printing Ltd of London
www.newtonprinting.com

For Mum and Dad

The Author

Malcolm Boyden began writing for *The Times* newspaper in August 2002. His career in journalism, however, started on the *Redditch Indicator*, where he won the Heart of England Journalist award in 1985. He later went on to work as sports editor of the *Birmingham Daily News* and sports sub editor on the *Daily Star*. For the last ten years he has presented his own afternoon radio show, which has an enormous following in the West Midlands. He is a double Sony award-winning radio presenter and a successful actor, his most recent role being the character of Lenny Cox in *Wallop Mrs Cox* at the Birmingham Rep. He has twice performed alongside Frank Bruno in pantomime and, this Christmas, will team up with Julian Clary in *Cinderella* at the Birmingham Hippodrome. Malcolm, who has also danced with the Royal Ballet, lives in Worcestershire with his wife Maxine and two sons Elliott and Oliver. He is an ardent fan of West Bromwich Albion Football Club. The **BRUM'S THE WORD** columns were written in a cupboard underneath his stairs! His first novel *Perfect* (another "under the stairs production") is due out in November.

Where it all began

Monday, May 23, 1977.

IT WAS ANDY GRAY'S fault. He didn't mean it, but he's definitely the one to blame.

It was spring 1977. The kids of the day were hooked on skateboarding, slime and Othello, the Chinese board game. On television, we were watching George and Mildred, Oh No! It's Selwyn Froggitt and Sale of the Century with Nicholas Parsons ('Live, from Norwich - it's the quiz of the week'). In the charts, Kenny Rogers was questioning a lady called Lucille about her timing, The Eagles were booking into the *Hotel California* and Rod Stewart was at number one with *The First Cut is the Deepest*. On the dance floor, those funky enough were learning *The Shuffle*, thanks to Van McCoy, while in football, Liverpool were crowned champions with a bit to spare and Don Revie was about to turn his back on England in favour of the United Arab Emirates.

For a 12-year-old West Bromwich Albion supporter, life was good. It was the last game of the season, a long-awaited local derby match against Aston Villa. The Baggies were in the ascendancy having just completed a successful first term back in the big time. Johnny Giles, "the messiah", was about to play his last game in English football.

As a "trainee" Albion die-hard, I had never set foot inside Villa Park before. The place immediately scared me to death. I was overawed by the size of the Holte End, the noise from the home fans in those days was enough to belittle the most ardent football follower. Already I was beginning to feel small - then, to rub salt into my wounds, Gray struck ... Not once, not twice but three times.

BRUM'S THE WORD

When his third hit the back of the net, a simple tap-in after the ball had rebounded against a hapless John Osborne in the Albion goal, the Aston Villa striker raised his arms to the heavens in triumph - and that was that. The writing was on the wall. Then, in a fateful twist, he turned and glared directly into my eyes for a split second. At that moment I knew that my goose was well and truly cooked. I became a man - a football man. It was the turning point in my life, and it was all his fault.

My head had been virtually rammed between the railings of the visitors' enclosure at the Witton End all evening. Even when Albion began to struggle, I'd put a brave face on things. At 12, you can afford to look on the bright side - I had only just stopped believing in Father Christmas. But Gray's sinister glance was the final straw. It was too much for me to bear. I immediately burst into tears, I felt myself going and could do nothing about it. The blonde haired, Scottish man in the claret and blue shirt had ruined my life. He'd demolished my team and then had the audacity to turn and look at me. To make matters worse, I was now making a complete fool of myself - crying my heart out in front of a crowd of 45,541.

I've often wondered why he picked on me. Malcolm Boyden, a run-of-the-mill West Midlands kid. For a moment, I was dumbstruck. It must have been similar to how the judges felt when Harvey Smith lobbed two fingers to the royal box after his clear round on Mattie Brown at the Hickstead Derby in 1971. In his defence, Gray, now enjoying fame and fortune as a Sky Television pundit, would never have known that I was on the edge. It probably wasn't even me he was looking at. But the damage was done.

Until then, I'd been largely unaffected by the cold-blooded, callous nature of what they call "the beautiful game". I had enjoyed a relatively easy ride. Suddenly, I was experiencing a nasty backlash, and it was hurting. Rod Stewart was right - the first cut was certainly the deepest.

BRUM'S THE WORD

Still sobbing, I tried to cover my face and stem the endless flow of tears with my hand-knitted "lucky" Albion bar-scarf that was hanging limply from my right wrist. A policeman patrolling the perimeter of the pitch spotted me. Very kindly, he bent down. "Don't worry son," he said, trying unsuccessfully to manoeuvre his gloved hand between the six-foot, spiked claret railings in order to pat my shoulder. "He didn't mean to upset you," he added, referring to the Scottish Villain. "Any road up, it's just a game."

I looked up in time to see Gray's wiggling backside disappear towards the corner flag. The policeman awkwardly removed his hand from inside the railings - he had no chance of getting close to my shoulder, and he knew it.

"You must never take this game to heart," the kindly copper said, still kneeling at my side. His words were calm and re-assuring. His voice was soft and gentle. I've long since wondered how I ever heard him above the din of the home supporters who were now ramming their boots against the wooden steps of the main stand. I waited patiently for a second, convinced that I was about to be comforted by a gem of football wisdom. "You remind me of my best mate," he said, "and you wouldn't want to take after him - he's a bastard. When his team lose, he goes home and beats his wife black and blue."

The bobby, realising I'd been somewhat let-down by his adult "advice", stood bolt upright. Folding his arms behind his back, he gave me a knowing nod and heartily hoofed it back towards the corner of the ground, where Gray was completing his final rear-end wiggle.

Of course, I was never going to turn into a wife beater on the kick of a ball. But I knew from that moment, when Andy Gray put the ball into the back of the net and stared me out - as if to say, "that one's for you Boyden, you 12-year-old Albion twerp." I knew from that moment that football had got me. I'd "taken the game to heart", fallen for it hook line and sinker. And when football gets you like that - it never, ever lets you go.

Nearly 30 years later, I was asked by Richard Whitehead at *The Times* to follow football in the West Midlands during a season that would historically witness Birmingham's big three standing shoulder to shoulder in the Barclaycard Premiership for the first time. I was to write a column, Brum's the Word, to reflect the mood of an area where the people still lived for the game, yet they'd been starved of success for so long that everybody had forgotten they existed at all.

I was reluctant at first. I'd worked with Richard 20 years earlier on the sports desk of the *Birmingham Daily News*, Europe's first free daily newspaper, and I knew I would be in safe hands. But I'd long since abandoned my journalistic career to present a daily show on BBC local radio. I was too busy dancing with the Birmingham Royal Ballet and taking tea with Lord Lichfield (He reckons he's my number one fan, which means I now count myself as being a broadcaster by Royal Appointment). I even appeared with Frank Bruno in pantomime. It was my job to land a left-right combination on him, twice a day for eight weeks over the Christmas period. We performed together for two years and he never punched me back, which, I thought, gave me the right to stake a valid claim for the world heavyweight boxing crown.

I ask you. How can any sports-mad male think about his notebook and pen when he's giving Bruno a good hiding twice a day in front of a packed house?

Besides, *The Times* is a daunting proposition. It's like a player receiving an international call-up after just three first-team games with Peterborough United. It's an FA Cup final for a 16-year-old striker who has just been plucked out of the Sunday league. It's the highest honour. I felt extremely unworthy.

Things began to change when the people at *The Times* explained that I was merely to use the game as my canvas - a blank sheet on which I would paint pictures of West Midlands people that feed on football. Those who "took it personally". Just like I did on May 23, 1977.

With that, I knew I was on home ground.

I was given complete freedom for the project, with the unstinting support of Keith Blackmore, the Head of Sport, David Chappell, the Sports Editor, Tim Hallissey, the Deputy Sports Editor and Tim Rice, the Saturday sports editor. Outside the newspaper's office, I was helped by Nigel Iskander and the photographers of News Team International, Dave Woodhall from the Aston Villa fanzine *Heroes and Villans,* Bob Matthews at Birmingham City, Phil Mepham and his team at Aston Villa, Tony Matthews, the West Bromwich Albion historian and Jenny Wilkes and John Platt at BBC WM.

Most of all, I'm indebted to Richard Whitehead who had the faith and trust to suggest me, that "funny little bloke" he used to work with all those years ago, to carry out the mission. He set me off on one of the most fruitful and enjoyable journeys of my entire career.

The folks you are about to read about are football people. It's that simple. Each one has their own personal tale to tell and I thank them for telling it so articulately to a complete stranger. I found them everywhere, sometimes in the most unusual haunts - a bingo hall in Bilston, a crematorium, the Birmingham Hippodrome Theatre, a church in Halesowen, Bromsgrove High Street, a black cab in the city centre and even a hostel for Bosnian refugees. Some were not easy to track down. But once I'd found them, I soon found that we all spoke the same language. We had all, foolishly, taken football to heart.

I remember having my photograph taken for the column on a blisteringly hot August day in 2002, just a week before the new season started. I was perched, gnome-like, on a large concrete ball next to the Floozie in the Jacuzzi, one of Birmingham's much-loved pieces of modern art in Victoria Square. The idea was to make me look like a frustrated football supporter.

"Look up to the heavens with pleading hands," the photographer said, trying to arrange his shot. I immediately outstretched my arms in what I considered to be a pleading gesture. I looked to the heavens, as instructed, wondering just what the next 40 weeks would bring. In truth, I was also questioning what I had let myself in for.

"Try to put a bit of expression into your face," the photographer insisted, re-focussing his lens as dozens of busy tourists and not-so-busy office workers milled past, some stopping to take in the unprompted and unexpected free side-show. "Look pained," the photographer shouted in desperation. "Think of somebody who has ruined your life."

I thought for a second - then the penny dropped. On the outside, I began to show pain. Inside, I was quietly saying to myself: "Thank you, Andy Gray. Thank you very much."

Boresville ready to go
Boom bang-a-bang

Saturday, August 17, 2002.

THE EUROVISION SONG CONTEST swung it.

On a barmy Brummie evening in May 1998, an Israeli transsexual named Dana International barked out the catchy *Viva La Diva* to see off stiff competition from 24 other nations (including the Swiss who notched nil points) and land first prize in the Continent's cheesiest talent show. Suddenly, Birmingham was back on the map. The "city of a thousand trades" had proved that it had a place in the modern world. Apparently there's an exclusive club in Small Heath where members still cross-dress to celebrate the landmark. Now, the Small Heath sisters are ready to swing again.

Even Sir Albert Bore, Birmingham's mild mannered yet much esteemed council chief, is rubbing his hands in glee at the prospect of his beloved city, recapturing its "Eurovision" sparkle, despite having to take a back seat while Manchester basked in the glory of the Commonwealth Games.

So, for the knockers who are writing Birmingham off, post-Manchester hysteria and National Stadium fiasco, beware… Football is about to put the Bucks Fizz into Boresville.

"In 1998 Birmingham was very much alive, like Manchester has been," Bore said. "We hosted the Eurovision Song Contest, the Lions convention and the G8 summit. Next year we've got the World Indoor Athletics Championships, the International Textile and Machinery Exhibition at the N.E.C - and, of course, football. There's no doubt, if all three teams can stay up this season, that will bring even greater recognition to the city - and greater recognition means more visitors."

Passion for passion, I don't know how the International Textile and Machinery Exhibition will match the Commonwealth Games, but football's a different kettle of fish. For the first time the "Birmingham three" - Blues, Villa and Albion - will battle it out side by side in the Premiership. Are you watching Manchester?

Even the Japanese want to swap the glittering Sapporo Dome for the throbbing nightlife of the Gas Street Basin.

Among the first to sign up for the brand new "Aston Villa Premiership weekends" (catchphrase, "turn 90 minutes of football into 48 hours of fun!") is a group of journalists from the Land of the Rising Sun, desperate to keep the World Cup spirit alive with a visit to Cadbury World.

And then there's Birmingham City versus Aston Villa - the musical. *A League Apart* premiers in Solihull next month. Malcolm Stent, a local comedian and lifelong Blues fan, is the author. "It's a Romeo and Juliet story based on four days in 1963 when Birmingham City won the League Cup over two legs against Aston Villa," he said.

The male love interest is a poor Blues fan, while the object of his desires comes from a rich mob of Villa supporters. (Just imagine Doug Ellis's daughter falling for Jasper Carrot's son pre-funky moped and you're on the right lines.) One of the songs goes: "When the Blues win a cup, they can call me up. Cause I'll be in heaven when Blues win the cup." Stent was there in 1963 - now he's reliving the drama on stage.

Meanwhile, on the field, they're preparing for the best Brummie soap storyline since Benny met Miss Diane. Let's take a whistlestop tour of the three clubs as they prepare for the big kick-off.

BOOM. Graham Taylor is hoping to make Aston not just a place to be, but *the* place to be. Even the fans are getting fed up of their team being looked on as "All dinner and no gong" merchants. Whoever said Britons don't complain enough, has surely never been to Villa Park on a match day. They've even been at it on the field. Taylor has labelled the club's last three goalkeepers as "the world's biggest moaners".

BANG. In central Birmingham, Steve Bruce has fallen with his bottom in the butter. Even he couldn't have forecast Premiership football so quickly. One Hall Green gentleman confessed he hasn't been so excited since he hit the "floating planet" to win a speed boat on The Golden Shot in 1974. Others think it's the equivalent to wafting half a pound of tuppenny rice and half a pound of treacle in the face of a weasel - they're waiting for the animal to go pop.

BANG. Just a few miles northwest, a corner of the Hawthorns straddles the Birmingham boundary, which wins them a place among the three musketeers. After a summer of discontent in the boardroom, the idolised Gary Megson has suddenly started to splash out. He's brought Sean Gregan from Preston. His qualities, according to Megson, include: "Personality and voice." One less than convinced fan mumbled: "If we wanted personality and voice we should have signed Tina Turner."

If all three survive, I'm prepared to bath naked with the Floozie in the Jacuzzi.

But the prospects are mouth watering. And, as the new Birmingham anthem states: "Forward in name, forward in heart. Every tomorrow is a brand new start."

I'm tempted to wish all three clubs the best of luck. But, according to the Russians, "Good luck is an eel in the pond of fools!" Now there's a cue for a Eurovision smash, if ever I heard one.

BRUM'S THE WORD

West Midlands Football Fever began to spread rapidly. The stars were queuing up to lavish praise on and declare their undying love for the "Birmingham Three". West Bromwich Albion came out head and shoulders above the other two in the "long lost supporters" stakes. Brookside darling, turned Celebrity Big Brother survivor and West End Musical star Claire Sweeney was first to "out herself" as a lifelong Throstle. "I love the Baggies," confessed the Scouse starlet, "but I also like Everton! Goodness only knows what I'll do when the two clubs play each other."

Rolling Stones guitarist Ronnie Wood was the next Baggie to tumble out of the closet. "My brothers started supporting them when they were young and I followed suit. I've still got a soft spot for them now," he said. "West Bromwich Albion were very big in the 1950s," he added, defending his surprising football revelation with one eye focussed on his fading street credibility. "It's a bit like my boys supporting Arsenal and Chelsea today," he reasoned.

The finest Baggie "new boy", however, was actor Ged Simmons, who played Detective Inspector Alex Cullen in the ITV drama The Bill. Simmons, brought up in Oxhill Road, Handsworth - just a lofty left-footed drive away from The Hawthorns - made it his personal mission to get his West Bromwich Albion mug in as many Bill shots as possible. In the end, it took over his whole working day. "At first I introduced the mug into Cullen's office as an extra prop - and to show a bit of allegiance to the team," he said. "Then, when I realised I was leaving the show, I began plotting how to give the mug as much exposure as possible. It became a bit of an obsession. By the end of my Bill stint it was appearing in an average of three scenes every episode." Finally, Simmons pulled off the ultimate mug coup. "I persuaded the director of my last scene to open with a close-up shot of the mug being packed away in a box," he said. "I'd finally made the mug a star."

Simmons' obsessive nature, where football is concerned, goes back a long way. "When I was a boy of eight, I got the autograph of Hughie Reed, Albion's outside right, seven times before, during and after one reserve match. He probably thought I was a nutter," he said.

Elvis and the fat man return to dreamland

Saturday, August 24, 2002.

A FLABBY GENT stands at the top of a small concrete staircase in Old Trafford's East Stand. It's been a struggle for him to make the climb, yet he's determined to pause for a second and gently drink it all in. His dress is horribly wrong for the occasion. An ill-fitting, stained grey jacket barely covers a cheesecloth shirt that might best be described as magnolia and faded pink. A small lapel badge is pinned awkwardly onto his breast pocket. It boasts "West Bromwich Albion FA Cup winners 1968". He's sweating like a glassblower's backside in the hot August sun.

You could have plucked him straight from the Black Country circa 1933. The same man, lolloping up Union Street after a hard day's grind at Salter's steelworks. Thirteen screaming kids are waiting at home. On the table, a plate piled high with faggots and peas - then five pints of Bathams Ale in the snug bar at the Bull and Bladder Public House.

"Row three," a 21st century football steward interrupts. "To your right, sir." The flabby gent stands his ground. It's his moment. From his lips you can hear the names Jason Roberts and Russell Hoult, but in his eyes you can see a dribbling Ronnie Allen, a charging Cyrille Regis and another of Jeff Astle's bullet headers crashing into the top corner of the net.

"To your right sir," the steward insists. "Hang on a minute lad," the Baggies man replies. "I've waited 16 years for this."

BRUM'S THE WORD

An over-excited, middle-aged lady, who resembles Mrs White, the cook in Cluedo, breaks the tension. She falls into the arms of her fellow fan. "I'm the one in the pink tent!" she wails. Her friend remembers. They spent three nights together, sharing a pavement outside The Hawthorns to secure their tickets for today. For them, it's an honour and a privilege to be here.

Across the way, the success-soaked home fans look on in bewilderment as a few bars of "My brother's shed is bigger than this" echoes from the away pen. Of course, it's rubbish - nobody has a shed bigger than Old Trafford.

But they've got a point. Old Trafford is no promised land. Indeed, for the success-starved supporters, emerging from that staircase to get their first real view of the stadium, their immediate sense of wonderment is almost immediately replaced by a feeling of let down. One by one you can see their faces drop. The place is monstrous yet heartless. There's nowhere near enough romance for it to be labelled the Theatre of Dreams. It has the ambience of a multi-screen cinema.

But on the first day of a season that they have spent more than a decade and a half waiting for, there's no need for a theatre. The travelling fans are already in dreamland. On day two, in the more elegant surroundings of Highbury, it's a similar story for Birmingham City. Although here, Elvis Presley has put in an unexpected appearance, 25 years after his death. He's resplendent in red jumpsuit and matching robe with an accompanying banner suggesting that the king of rock'n'roll was a closet Bluenose.

Elvis is given a guard of honour by his makeshift "entourage" as he squeezes through the turnstiles bellowing the opening lines of *Keep Right on to the End of the Road*, the Blues' signature tune. "Mr Presley is now entering the stadium," one of his gang announces. (Apparently, the same mob dressed as characters from the Wizard of Oz on the opening day of last season. On that occasion, Elvis was the Tin Man).

Elvis, also known as Tim Woodfield from Solihull ("My mum's making me a royal blue jumpsuit for our first home game") feasts his eyes upon the magical surroundings for a moment. He then takes an imaginary microphone in his right hand. *It's Now or Never*, he sings to the delighted massed ranks behind him.

Back at Old Trafford, the fans are holding tight. Their first taste of paradise is proving to be a white-knuckle rollercoaster ride. First there's a standing ovation as Baggie Bird races from the Old Trafford tunnel. Next, gasps and roars as Albion appear to be matching Manchester United stride for stride. After the break an endless stream of world-class players haul themselves off the bench and into the action as Sir Alex Ferguson attempts a reshuffle. "Bring the sodding lot on," one over confident Albion supporter yells.

There's intrigue as David Beckham wanders over to take a corner. Nobody has ever seen him this close before "in the flesh". He smiles heartily and, in return, receives a gentle ripple of applause. It's the fans way of acknowledging his acknowledgement. There's another verse of Psalm 23 - the Albion anthem. "Through pastures green, he leadeth me," the devoted sing, looking to the heavens for divine intervention. It doesn't come. Heroic Hoult, the Albion goalkeeper, is finally thwarted by Ole Gunnar Solskjaer. "He can't save them all," a bare-chested father whispers to his inconsolable youngster.

Two goals in the first 24 minutes at Arsenal leave Elvis and his acolytes even more desperate. "Seaman, Seaman give us a goal," they plead to the England goalkeeper who was a Bluenose himself the last time the sides met. It doesn't come... momentarily, the King is all shook up. For Heartbreak Hotel, read Heartbreak Highbury.

BRUM'S THE WORD

In the end, both away teams bravely surrendered with a man apiece sent off. After Aston Villa's defeat by Liverpool earlier on Sunday, it's nil points for the three Birmingham sides and no goals scored (the bookies are quoting 150-1 they all go down). But the results were of almost secondary importance. Sometimes even the world's greatest football league needs a wake-up call. This season it's coming from the West Midlands' "new two"… It's not just the best league in the world, it's also the most magical.

Take it from Phil Neville, who was kind enough to give me his Old Trafford post match thoughts … Not THE Phil Neville, Manchester United and England (Brother of Times' columnist Gary), but Phil Raymond Neville - a lorry driver from Walsall.

Scarcely able to hold back the tears, he squealed: "One nil with ten men. Excellent. Thirty years I've been following Albion and I'm so proud. Russell Hoult - England's number one. Super. Fantastic." With that, he turned to boing one last time.

Others were not so observant. Peter Drury, the ITV commentator, later summed up the Old Trafford occasion as a "routine" United win. He'd hopelessly missed the bus.

If Drury had spared a second to glance over to one small corner of Old Trafford, he'd have witnessed a rarity in British football 2002 - die-hard loyalty and blind passion. It's what the game was made for. And when the money dries up, it will be the only thing it has left to feed on.

You try telling the flabby gent or Elvis Presley that last weekend was routine. Even Mrs White the Cluedo cook had her loyalty repaid with a memorable day out, although she left Old Trafford with a face like a chip that had been trodden on. "I'll have to start thinking about queuing for the Arsenal game now," she said.

It looks like the pink tent is going to be a permanent fixture outside The Hawthorns this season.

* *Gary Megson, the West Bromwich Albion manager, refused to let his players get carried away on their first Premier League away-day. He warned them that he would not tolerate "shirt swapping" at the end of the game. Megson told his players that if they wanted David Beckham's jersey they would have to visit the Merry Hill Shopping Centre in Dudley to purchase their own. "We want to respect our Premiership opponents - not fall in love with them," he warned.*

* *David Morgan, via email, writes: "I really enjoyed your article in* The Times *because I could relate to the scene. I could have been that bloke looking around Old Trafford recalling the glory days of the past and hoping against all hope for a bright future. Your words sent a magical shiver down my spine. People who have brought themselves into the game because it's fashionable will never get that 'shiver down the spine' feeling because that sort of passion and loyalty can only be born within you. When you look at Albion and Blues you see a mix of people - rich and poor - standing side by side with a common passion for football. That is what I call success and if we lose every game, I'll still be there in 2003-04. Keep up the good work."*

* *Kerry Davey, via email from New York, writes: "I have just seen your article in* The Times. *It's one of the most fantastic things I have ever read. I'm a very frustrated Albion fan living in New York yet your James Joyce style had me walking towards Old Trafford with the fans. The match for me was almost as dreamlike as your article. Sat in a cool, air-conditioned room at 10am - the temperature outside was 110 - I felt the hairs on the back of my neck stand with excitement and pride when I heard the away* *supporters singing "The Lord's My Shepherd". Now, as I reach for my bagel, you've got me thinking of faggots and peas followed by a half time balti pie."*

Though the carnival is over, I will love you till I die

Saturday, August 31, 2002.

POP LEGENDS can tell your life story in a line - it's their trade. In this case, the Buxom Australian girl in the white thigh-length boots summed it all up in 1965. "The carnival is over," she sang to her enchanted teenage disciples. When the Seekers visited Birmingham for their farewell concert at the Symphony Hall last year, Judith Durham recalled those halcyon days of the mid-1960s. "I knew it would be a hit," she said. "I bought the boots for when we got to number one. They're still at home now, although they're starting to go yellow. I'm thinking of throwing them out."

With a touch of sadness, she looked wistfully into the distance; it was the end of the road, but the memories were so sweet. "The carnival is over....that's how we're feeling now," she said before taking her final bow.

I know what she means. Within a fortnight, the carnival for West Bromwich Albion and Birmingham City has come to a crushing end, while Aston Villa are left with an all-too-familiar feeling of anti-climax. Bookmakers have slashed odds on all three getting relegated from 150-1 to just 17-1. Villa at least got off the mark on Wednesday and Blues picked up a point at Goodison. But at 2-7 for the drop, Albion are the shortest priced favourites for relegation since the Premiership began, despite their wickedly difficult first three fixtures.

Gary Megson, the Albion manager, has told his players to behave like top golfers. "The ones that are successful are those who hole the putts," he said. At Villa, meanwhile, Graham

Taylor has adopted the role of Colin Crompton, legendary MC of the Wheeltappers and Shunters Social Club. Crompton would ring his bell and ask members to "give order" for Canadian Tina the baton-twirling temptress from Barnsley. Taylor is using similar words to appeal for calm at his club. He has described Villa Park as a political minefield. "There seem to be hidden agendas all over the place here," he said. "The biggest problem we've got is to try and settle everybody down. Both on and off the pitch."

The carnival is most certainly over.

Scratching around for a glimmer of good news has been like trying to find a harbourmaster for land-locked Birmingham. Yet, out of the gloom, an unlikely ray of sunshine has appeared in the unmistakable form of the Aston Villa chairman: Herbert Douglas Ellis.

Ellis, often referred to by his chilling nickname, Deadly, is enjoying a sudden and quite unexpected popularity surge, thanks to a pair of boxer shorts, a mug - and a clock. It's hard to swallow. Especially when you study his record of two League Cup wins in the 20 years since his return to the boardroom and the regular choruses of "Ellis Out" that echo around Villa Park. But it's true.

From out of the claret and blue, an "Ellis In" campaign has emerged. Incredibly, there's even an "Ellis In" website - www.ellisin.co.uk - that is hoping to do a roaring trade in Deadly merchandise - that's where the boxer shorts, mugs and clocks come in. The Ellis clock is tastefully designed with the words "Ellis In" across the face, and, if you order more than 25 pairs of Ellis boxer shorts, you can get a 35 per cent discount. A "new and exclusive range" of Ellis beach hats are also on special offer this month.

The website, full title: "Ellis In - in support of a Great Chairman" includes an "Ellis-O-Meter", which questions the frustrated faithful on their loyalty to the club. How far the meter swings depends upon how fans answer questions such as: "Do you think the job of a supporter is to moan and rant about the chairman or get behind the team and support the players?"

Another page gives "five reasons to applaud Ellis". These include the belief that he won't bankrupt the club in search of success and that all "Ellis Out" campaigns are doomed to failure. Unfortunately, they have overlooked the most startling Deadly tit-bit, his claims to have invented the revolutionary bicycle kick when he was playing for a British XI alongside the likes of Stanley Matthews and Tom Finney. "Funny that," recalls Ron Atkinson, a former Villa manager. "He told me he played in goal for Southport!"

The "In" crowd have even set up a question and answer section in which one "out merchant" calling himself Gobsmaked asks: "Are you for real?" Another states: "You are the laughing stock of Villa Park. Are you D. Ellis?" Others might question whether the man behind the site was taking Ellis D. The truth is, the driving force behind the campaign prefers to stay anonymous, "in case of death threats." Trying to uncover the ringleader is like trying to unmask the infamous Tiswas Phantom Flan Flinger.

But the new bread of Ellis fans are not afraid to stick doggedly to their guns: "Get a life," they rant back at the cynical. "He saved the club from financial ruin and brought us to second place in the old Division One in 1989," they add, describing their quest as "A rational response to the irrational hate campaign against the Villa chairman."

It is, therefore, with great pride that I'm able to announce to the footballing world that all is well in the Midlands. Well, at Aston Villa anyway. To be more precise, in the Aston Villa boardroom - but at least it's a start.

And, of course, having unearthed such a gem amid such gloom, it will come as no surprise that I've also found

Birmingham's harbourmaster. Albert Rooke has held the job for the last 15 years, but he will be retiring in April. The man has become a living legend in the world of British harbour masters, dealing mainly with Birmingham's inland waterways. The city has more canals than Venice - it's one of our proudest boasts (The other is that Quinton is the highest point between the Brecon Beacons in Wales and the Russian Urals - if you look in a Westerly direction.)

Albert was a fanatical Villa fan, but he "lost interest in 1982" - about the same time that Herbert Douglas Ellis arrived back at the club. He now prefers to spend his Saturday afternoons watching Boldmere Saint Michaels in the Midland Alliance and has even got a place on the "Mikes" board. Imagine that. A living legend holding court in a football boardroom (Mr Ellis would do well to take note).

The only problem for British Waterways will be how to replace Albert, and what to buy him for his forthcoming retirement.

I know where to get my hands on a pair of yellowing thigh-length boots, formerly owned by Judith Durham, but I don't suppose he'd be interested. Perhaps a Doug Ellis clock would be more up his street?

A classic free kick
at cow corner

Saturday, September 7, 2002.

JOHN MOONEY has the look of a man waiting to hook a duck for his youngest son at Wilson's travelling fun fair. The next few moments are not going to alter his life, but he is desperate to make a fist of it. Mooney is teeing up to take a free kick some 25 yards out. The tension mounts. His mate Colm O'Laoi, who is in goal, checks that his one-man wall is in position. With a gentle stroke of his luscious right boot, Mooney places the ball sweetly into the top corner of the net, leaving the hapless goalkeeper stranded.

"Bugger me! I thought it was going over," O'Laoi says. "He's bent it like Beckham."

Mooney knows all about Beckham because he is an avid Manchester United fan living a stone's throw away from Old Trafford. But his elegant strike will get no headlines. He is playing with a ball that cost less than a tenner, shooting at a goal that he found dumped in a nearby hedge. If you glance 500 yards to the right you see The Belfry golf club. That's why the three of them are here. Mooney, O'Laoi and their "one-man wall" Mark Twomey, work for a company that make golf buggies.

Their home until the Ryder Cup finishes at the end of the month is a field at Middleton House Farm, over the road from the course. They live in two three-berth caravans. In a small cardboard box they have a silver teapot and a bag of sugar. Next to the box is a bin bag bulging with empty beer tins. The only "spectators" to witness that great free kick is a herd of priceless Holstien Fresian Cows, kept away from the action by an electric fence.

Glance 500 yards to the left and the priceless England squad arrive at Bodymoor Heath, Aston Villa's training ground, in preparation for the friendly against Portugal at Villa Park today. Mooney, O'Laoi and Twomey gather their ball and stare in awe. Their moment is interrupted briefly by "Romeo", the dog they've adopted from the farm and rechristened in honour of the new Beckham baby. His coat is grey and matted, he's getting on in years, but he wants to play on. He will have to wait. Through the trees the lads spot Sven-Goran Eriksson leading his squad off the team bus. The players have football on their minds, but as the clouds gather over a less than welcoming Bodymoor Heath, their faces seem to suggest that they are really thinking: "I'm a celebrity, get me out of here".

I can sympathise. I've never had a great deal of affection for training grounds. As a 12-year-old I went to watch Scottish international Willie Johnston train with West Bromwich Albion. It was drizzling and, by the time I arrived, he had gone. I wrote a poem at school entitled: *I went to see Willie - but Willie wasn't there.* The first two lines have stayed with me, almost engraved on the back of my mind. "I went to see Willie but he'd departed/There was just a field with netless goals/It left me broken hearted".

Since then I have stayed well clear. Training grounds make you feel small and insignificant. You're too close to the players for comfort. On the training pitch heroes become humans... and that is not right for a true fan. At football stadiums, you know your place. The dearly beloved gather to pay homage to the untouchables. On the training ground, the barriers are down. Strict lines separating the worshippers from the worshipped become blurred and the atmosphere is awkward.

Still, work for the England squad soon begins. It's football, but there's no romance. That will be left until 3.55pm today when Ronald Samm of the Birmingham Opera Company will sing the British and Portugese national anthems before the match. He has been dragged away from Birmingham's Artsfest, an extravaganza that's taking place all weekend across the city (An annual event whose marketing slogan is "One city, two days, 350 events, no charge."). Samm is one of the performers alongside a pair of pantomime dames, the Ukulele Orchestra of Britain and, by way of a climax, a French street theatre group waltzing with an inflatable "goddess of love" in Centenary Square with Adrian Goldberg of BBC's Watchdog providing the commentary.

Back at Bodymoor Heath, the England circus continues, and the big guns are out in force. For a moment, training is halted as Doug Ellis, the Aston Villa chairman, wanders onto the pitch, seemingly oblivious to the hustle and bustle around him. Gently stooping with hands in pockets, he arrives on the centre spot to discuss matters with the England head coach. On the sidelines, Villa assistant manager John Deehan urges his young son to stand behind the rope. Resplendent in red England shirt, digital camera in hand, Deehan junior is getting a little over excited.

Things are hotting up at the makeshift caravan site, too. Our three friends are standing on top of their white Transit van, gazing in amazement through binoculars as the crème de la crème of the English game are put through their paces. Finally, as the players finally head off towards another press conference and a quiet night at the nearby New Hall Hotel, Mooney, O'Laoi and Twomey get ready for a pint in the Dog and Doublet.

They sit on canvas angling chairs, mulling over the unexpected events of the day while surveying the charred remains of last night's barbeque of spicy chicken wings.

Before they head off, there is time for one last kickabout. Romeo the dog leaps around like a gazelle sensing another slice of action.

"The ball is the first thing we brought," Mooney said. "It's saved our lives," he adds, humping another chip goalwards as Sven's battle bus passes the slightly ajar five-bar farm gates. Like the Holstien Fresians, one or two players momentarily turn their heads to view the action.

"Marvellous," adds O'Laoi. "It's not every day the England team turns up to train on your doorstep. It's hard to believe it's happened."

But it happened all right …. Once upon a time, in the Midlands.

Woofle dust, woofle dust, wherefore art thou?

Saturday, September 14, 2002.

WOOFLE DUST. It's what the good fairy produces when she lifts her magic wand. Sparks fly and a million stars appear from out of nowhere - that's woofle dust.

Singer/songwriter Harvey Andrews has witnessed woofle dust firsthand. In the 1960s he wandered into the Jug of Punch folk club at Digbeth Civic Hall. The atmosphere was tense. Ian Campbell, the club owner and father of UB40 brothers Ali and Robin, was in a smoke-filled corner of the room, roasting a scruffy young American who had turned up a week late.

With a flea in his ear, the boy was finally allowed to play four songs. He began to sing and, at once, the small crowd fell under his spell. His name was Paul Simon - he'd sprinkled the lucky Digbeth few with pure woofle dust.

"Woofle dust is magic," Andrews said. "And it often appears in football. When Aston Villa beat Charlton 11-0 and Gerry Hitchens scored five goals before half time, I got the same feeling as watching Paul Simon at the Jug of Punch. Every time Hitchens touched the ball it went in. Remarkable."

Being a Birmingham City fan living just eight minutes walk from Villa Park, football woofle dust has been in short supply for Andrews, but he's expecting a good smattering of it on Monday night when his beloved Blues meet Aston Villa in the first league derby between the two arch enemies for 15 years. Across the city, in leafy Solihull, a musical based on the intense rivalry (which often borders on sheer hostility) between the clubs, is performing to packed houses. It's one way of getting fans in the mood for the real thing.

Called *A League Apart*, the show is written by comedian Malcolm Stent. Andrews penned the songs. It's a *Romeo and Juliet*-type love story about two Birmingham families from opposite sides of the tracks - the poor Coggins clan from Small Heath who support Birmingham, and the upper-crust Pearsons from Sutton Coldfield who favour the Villa. Stent plays Ted Coggins, whose son Billy falls for Sandra, the Pearsons' daughter. The action takes place during May 1963 when Blues beat Villa 3-1 over two legs to win their only football honour - the League Cup.

A quartet of Midlands football luminaries in Joe Gallagher, Chris Nicholl, John Deehan and Bobby Thompson, who scored the Villa goal in that 1963 encounter, were part of a "star-studded" first night audience. Gallagher smiled as Ted Coggins sat in his grotty armchair devouring a match report from the first leg of the epic encounter. "I sometimes think you love Birmingham City more than me," Betty, his long-suffering wife, rants. Ted looks distastefully at his other half and barks: "I love the Villa more than I love you."

Ted's big number in the musical goes: "When the Blues win a cup, they can call me on up. 'Cause I'll be in heaven when the Blues win a cup."

"It's a song of passion and yearning. A Villa fan could never write a song like that," said Andrews, who began his love affair with music in 1962 when a mate lent him the first two Bob Dylan albums. "I fell for Dylan and his music instantly. I didn't come out of my bedroom for 24 hours," he said. When he finally emerged he knew every word of every song.

His love affair with Birmingham City goes back even further. He opened the first souvenir shop at St Andrew's, and often sang to warm up the crowd before an important Blues game. One song, he remembers, was a version of *Bye Bye Blackbird* entitled *Bye Bye Rangers* before a 1965 League Cup match with Queen's Park Rangers. Unfortunately, his performance that day was brought to an abrupt halt when two opposing fans ran onto the pitch and made off with the microphone.

Harvey, who had a number two hit in New Zealand with *Hey Sandy* in the early 1970s, reckons that supporting Blues has been reflected in his music. "Never being a top dog colours your whole outlook on life," he says, citing Tony Hancock as the "classic" Bluenose. Ted Coggins has a touch of Hancock about him, too. Alone on the stage, he gazes solemnly at the auditorium and, with the look of a tortured man, pleads: "Did we do something wrong? 'Cause it's taking so long." His song goes on: "It's always the Villa and never the Blues. But you're born to your team - it's not something you choose. They need your support so you never refuse. Even though, in the cup, the Blues always lose."

Back in the real world, security guard Tom Roberts, of Druids Heath, has told a sorry tale that might well have graced an episode of *Hancock's Half Hour.* Apparently, he roared so loudly when Birmingham notched their first Premiership goal of the season that his pet parrot Charlie died of a heart attack. Mr Roberts wasn't even watching the game, just monitoring Teletext in his semi-darkened front room. "I was jumping around screaming 'yes' when my wife told me Charlie had collapsed in his cage," Tom said sadly. "The shock of my scream was obviously too much for his heart," he added. "He hadn't been very well lately." The match had put paid to his much-loved pet. But he was happy with the points. That's passion for you.

It's the same passion and desire that Harvey Andrews wrote about for the musical - and it's why Villa could sink without trace on Monday evening. I'm convinced that Graham Taylor's side will wilt under the pressure of the occasion.

When Blues met Villa in March 1986, football's top division was called the Canon League. Blues won 3-0 with a goal from Steve Witton and a Wayne Clarke brace. I asked Harvey Andrews what a repeat of that result would mean to the Blues faithful on Monday - he thought for a moment. Then slowly, a broad smile seemed to take ten years off his face.

"Double woofle dust," he replied.

Monday, September 16, 2002.

Double woofle dust!
BIRMINGHAM CITY 3, ASTON VILLA 0
Morrison 31, Enckelman og 76, Horsfield 83.

* 'Cannock Wolves' Steve, via email, writes: "I was fascinated to find out that Harvey Andrews opened the first souvenir shop at St Andrew's. Throughout the seventies, he was to be found at Molineux running OUR club store behind the old North Bank. It's interesting to recall the stock carried by a typical souvenir shop in those days. There were no items of clothing except for the obligatory scarves (barred, 'university' or silk). If one wanted a replica shirt, the place to go was a sports outfitters.

"Instead we were offered such delights as key rings, mugs and big tin badges. Possibly, however, the most quintessential bit of 'tat' was a plastic sleeve, emblazoned with a Wolves logo in which to slip your back-pocket comb... Whether the comb was included or not, has been lost in the mists of time."

Adding the Finnish touch to Blue Monday

Saturday, September 21, 2002.

"UUSI PAIVA UUSI ALKU!" It's a popular Finnish blessing. Roughly translated, it means: "A new day shows a new way". It's a simple message, given by Finns to fellow countrymen who are down on their luck. When Peter Enckelman, the Aston Villa goalkeeper, steps out at Villa Park to face Everton tomorrow, the whole nation should whisper a collective: "Uusi Paiva Uusi Alku".

It's the least he deserves. Enckelman's suffered a "weekus horribilis". His goalkeeping gaffe during Monday's remarkable second city derby against Birmingham City has grabbed the imagination of the nation - and split the West Midlands in half.

Birmingham fans are still basking in the glory of their night to remember. Some have started a campaign to get the word "Enckelman" into the *Oxford English Dictionary*. The submission would read something like this: "Enckelman (Doing an Enckelman): To blunder or fluff to the amusement and amazement of others." More imaginative Bluenoses are looking to the big screen. They are relishing the prospect of a spoof superhero blockbuster, where the lead character goofs at the crucial moment - after *Superman* and *Spiderman,* they think the stage is set for *Enckelman - the movie.*

Elsewhere, there has been a tremendous wave of sympathy for the Villa goalkeeper, who was born in the town of Turku, Finland's oldest city (a seaside town, labelled by tour operators as "the gateway to Europe"). One middle-aged lady from

BRUM'S THE WORD

Wolverhampton phoned my radio show out of the blue, desperate to cook him the traditional Finnish dish of *Liha pullat perunamuusi ja lanttu laatikko* (pork meat balls with mashed potato and swede - very popular at Christmas). She was hoping to deliver it personally to Enckelman's luxury bachelor pad in the city centre. "I want to make him feel warm inside," she said.

More serious observers point to the footballer's tremendous calm in brushing off the unwanted attention of "that" moron. Enckelman's supreme professionalism in the face of provocation of the vilest kind may have prevented a riot. Local newspapers have been besieged by letters from irate fans, demanding: "Where were the police? Where were the stewards?" Others are insisting on a custodial sentence for the "nutter in the baseball cap who gave the Villa man a slap".

Then there's the undeniable truth that Enckelman's mistake masked the two real talking points of the evening. Firstly, by manager Graham Taylor's own admission, his Villa players don't know the rules of the game. Secondly, and far more importantly, Villa are in the midst of an appalling decline. The claret and blue flag wavers can easily swallow a "freak accident" that will go down in football folklore. The fact that their team are now the third largest football club in the West Midlands is far harder to take.

Followers of West Bromwich Albion and Birmingham City are, naturally, only too happy to ram it down their throats. Albion are now seventh in the Premiership. A young car park attendant could hardly contain his excitement after their latest victory against Southampton. "Three wins in a row - above Manchester United! That's knocking on the door of Europe, isn't it?" he asked before whipping off his green fluorescent jacket and inexplicably bursting into a verse of *Me and my Shadow* before driving home with a beaming smile. Believe me, the Baggies ARE in seventh heaven.

Then there was Monday night. You could sense something special was about to happen before the game. The bedraggled elderly gentleman who spends most of his time standing in the same spot outside the players' entrance was unusually tense. With his trademark brown leather satchel, wooden crutches and ghastly 1950s blue and white bobble hat, he confessed to one lady: "I've had it coming out of both ends all day!" Scarcely able to control his loose-fitting false teeth, the Blues old-timer had summed it up a treat.

Inside St Andrew's, the din was deafening. The stand at the Tilton Road End shook with noise. Next to me, Alan Kirk, an English teacher at Handsworth Grammar School for Boys, arrived late and flustered. He whipped off his tie, arched his back and, with his mouth wide open, like a clown waiting to receive a ping pong ball on a fairground stall, he roared *Keep Right on to the End of the Road* with the gusto of a soloist at the "Last Night of the Proms". It's funny how football can transform you in an instant.

Strangely, nobody really saw the Enckelman incident in full. When the opposition have a throw-in deep inside their own half, the football fan's mind subconsciously takes a breather. English teacher Kirk looked at the ground. "We just can't get hold of the ball," he mumbled. Behind me, a nervy youngster tapped furiously on his digital watch. "I'm sure the flipping thing has stopped." He was desperate for Blues to hang on to their slim lead in the face of a growing Villa onslaught.

Then, for a split second, time did stop. Suspended in a moment of sheer disbelief. Thousands of heads looked up as the ball had bounced limply over the line. Humiliated to a man, the Villa fans began to leave the ground almost immediately, less than 200 were still in their seats at the final whistle, yet still they were taunted mercilessly by chants of "Enckelman's a Bluenose" and "Can we play you every week?".

When the match was over, you could reach out and touch the unmitigated delight of the home fans. "Wait!" one father said to his young daughter. Her nose was painted blue for the occasion. She wanted to make for the exit, it was past her bedtime and she had school in the morning. But dad was insistent. "Look at it," he urged her, pointing at a now empty pitch. "You'll remember this for the rest of your life."

Outside the ground, the elderly man was in his usual place outside the players' entrance. Nobody knows if he ever goes in - tonight nobody cared. With one crutch thrust into the air, he declared through dancing dentures: "If this is heaven, roll on death!"

In Peter Enckelman's case... If this is hell - roll on Everton.

***

THE BLUENOSE DICTIONARY

*Encircle v.tr. 1 (usu. foll. by with) surround, encompass. 2 form a circle around, **encirclement** n.*

Enckelman v. to blunder or fluff to the amusement and amazement of others. Doing an Enckelman. See ASTON VILLA.

Encl. Abbr. 1 enclosed. 2 enclosure.

***

* An ashen-faced Peter Enckelman was rolled out by Villa officials to face the press on the morning after his mistake. In broken English, he said: "Controlling the ball should have been the easiest thing to do in the world, but it was a blunder. I just want to apologise to the Villa supporters for

it. I knew there was going to be a fuss, but not this much - really. Goalkeepers need to be crazy and mentally strong. The first local derby for 15 years is not the game to make that sort of mistake. Probably my worst moment in football? Yes. Nothing even comes close to it."

* Peter Madeley, via email, writes: "Whilst I enjoy your articles in The Times, *I feel you are a little premature in proclaiming Aston Villa as "the third largest club in the West Midlands". Barely a week after the humiliation at St Andrew's, Villa are above both Blues and Albion in the Premiership. Your comments demonstrate perfectly how short-termism has become the norm in football these days. Villa are indeed in a period of decline while Blues are enjoying the heady heights of the Premiership for the first time. This does not mean that they are suddenly a bigger and more illustrious club than Villa. It will be interesting to see just how big Blues are come the end of the season when, I can assure you, they will be heading back to their regular birth in the First Division!"*

The day the earth moved

Monday, September 23, 2002.

AN EARTHQUAKE MEASURING 4.8 on the Richter Scale hit the West Midlands, and became headline news across the country. The epicentre was in Lower Gornal, deep in the heart of the Black Country, but tremors were felt across England and Wales. There were reports that the famous Crooked House pub in Brick Kiln Lane had straightened out. An elderly couple in Dudley had the shock of their lives when their bed began to roll across an uncarpeted bedroom floor on its castors, crashing into a newly built en-suite shower room. One woman in Tividale was devastated when her goldfish bowl toppled off the sideboard, leaving the pet fish floundering on the recently raked shag-pile carpet in her Bloxwich home.

Work began on making souvenir Richter Scales for the forthcoming Walsall Illuminations, tastefully decorated with the words "Lower Gornal - earthquake capital of the world" inscribed on the side. Local man Keith Middleton set up an earthquake appeal for the people of the Black Country.

"On the clothing front, we have a shortage of donkey jackets, flat caps and balaclavas," he said. "Food is also in short supply and again we are asking the people of Great Britain to be generous. In particular we are looking for faggots, chitlings, spam, grey peas and pigs' pudding.

"Many of the folk affected are also animal lovers - therefore we are also asking for spare pigeon and whippet food."

Tchaikovsky and Dion putting their best feet forward

Saturday, September 28, 2002.

IN THE FAIRYTALE LAND of the pirouette and the *pas de deux*, he is the undisputed king - revered by most as the best in the world. But, sat in his dark green office, which has the ambience of Victorian parlour complete with an antique pink *chaise longue*, and his grandmother's imposing wardrobe in the corner, David Bintley CBE, artistic director and choreographer of the Birmingham Royal Ballet (BRB), has something more pressing on his mind - Aston Villa.

The Villa mug on his desk is a giveaway. The latest edition of the club's fanzine, *Heroes and Villains,* sits on top of three huge red books. They contain the musical scores to *Cyrano de Bergerac,* his next project. He'll get stuck into them when he's finished reading the thoughts of Villa fan Ranting Robert. If more proof of his allegiance was needed, there is the shelf full of birthday cards. One contains a picture of Peter Enckelman, the Villa goalkeeper, with his head in his hands. "To the birthday boy" is scrawled underneath. Bintley "celebrated" his birthday the day after Villa lost to Birmingham City - he still can't bring himself to talk about it.

There's no need to. The unassuming genius is having a "contented day". His new ballet, *Concert Fantasy,* set to the music of his all time hero Pyotr Ilyich Tchaikovsky, is due to open at the Birmingham Hippodrome on Wednesday week.

More importantly, Villa have beaten Everton 3-2, with the winning goal coming from Dion Dublin, a ballet fanatic and Hippodrome regular. "I once asked him to appear in one of my productions, but he was worried about what the lads might think," Bintley said in all seriousness. Then, pausing for a second, he smiled: "I might still persuade him … I might still."

For David Bintley the beautiful art and the beautiful game go hand in hand. On a cork noticeboard in front of him, he has his "squad" - Principals, soloists, first artists and artists - 59 in all. To the right is his fixture list, Bintley's dates for the forthcoming season, which kicks off with his new piece. It needs to do well. After two years away from the theatre while it was refurbished, the Royal Ballet is horribly out of pocket.

"I've adored Tchaikovsky's music for 20 years and I've been figuring out how to put a ballet to it," Bintley, who admits he's delighted with his latest creation, said. "It's very classical and has a lot of quality, although it's cost us next to nothing," he added. "For the customs we've just tarted up some old tutus, but it looks great."

He's making magic on a shoestring budget. It's the formula every football manager is searching for. And Bintley is only too happy to compare his work to that of a soccer boss. His training ground is the BRB's rehearsal studio, his arena is the theatre, his FA Cup Final is every first night. "It's very similar," he said. "First I have to pick my starting line-up, it's called casting. In a company like this I've got squad members who I've brought on from schoolboy level. Others are imports who have come in at the top to add a bit of glamour. Then, over a season, I have to cope with injuries. I have to consider who I've got on the bench and who I can bring in. If I haven't got strength in depth I can end up with a poor show."

Bintley was brought up on Huddersfield Town, his local team. His heroes were Frank Worthington, Trevor Cherry - and Rudolph Nureyev. Now he worships Tchaikovsky whose picture is pinned to that noticeboard. "It has to be," he said. "We're working together!" Also on the board is Duke Ellington, Michael Schumacher - "Because I can't stand him." - And me! Malcolm Boyden. I also danced with Bintley's Royal Ballet in a charity show, *The Cracked Nut* - and he likes to be reminded of his favourite performers.

His is the story of a real life Billy Elliott. It began when, at the age of 6, he performed in a black and white minstrel show for his local Sunday School and became instantly stage struck. Within months he followed his sister, in enrolling for Audrey Spencer's Dance School. "A remarkable woman," he said. "She taught 300 kids in one room on the third floor of a shabby building up an alley."

At the age of 11, he was earmarked as the new Tommy Steele, but he wanted far more. Bintley was told he wasn't good enough to make it as a ballet dancer but that merely fired his enthusiasm. After school, he caught three buses to get to the Dorothy Stevens Academy in Halifax, often returning home after midnight. On Saturday he would travel to Manchester for more training, arriving back just in time to set off to Leeds Road if Huddersfield were playing at home. Despite the fights and name-calling at school, he finally made it to the Royal Ballet School.

Bintley breaks off to show me a black and white picture on his office wall. It's him as a younger man, baring an uncanny resemblance to Manchester United striker Ole Gunnar Solskjaer. ("Most people say I now look like Robin Williams," he confessed). He's receiving an award from his mentor, Dame Ninette de Valois, founder of the Royal Ballet. He respectfully calls her "Madame". Within seconds he's back to Aston Villa. "Here's the great thing," he says. "Our programme this year means I'm only going to miss one home game." His delight turns to disappointment in an instant. "But that game is Birmingham City at home!" It's the one he and seven-year-old son Gabriel ("He's a real Villain - it's his club!") desperately want to see.

He views every Villa game as if it were a ballet and although he fears that the present team is lacking in imagination, he is optimistic for the future. At the moment, his "Principal" is Darius Vassell. "When he's working well, his elegance is dazzling," he said with a twinkle in his eye.

Meekly, I suggest the possibility of bringing football to the stage in a new ballet. He's intrigued. Then enlightened. "You've given me an idea there," he said deep in thought. "Sport. It's a great theme for a triple bill," his creative juices are starting to flow. "Yes," he said. Both eyes twinkle now. "Leave that one with me!"

My idea, I feel, is in safe hands.

Astle is King

Monday, September 30, 2002.

LARRY GRAYSON AND JEFF ASTLE. Two of the most influential men in the life of John Mainwaring - West Midland musician, friend of Buzz Aldrin, the second man on the moon, and professional David Bowie impersonator.

Mainwaring, a staunch West Bromwich Albion supporter, who was born "at a Bloxwich maternity home in the middle of a thunderstorm", is hoping to stage a one-man musical play dedicated to the life of Grayson, the entertainer famed for his catchphrases "shut that door" and "have a gay day". He's made a healthy living impersonating Bowie for the last ten years, and became Aldrin's "buddy" during a star-studded film premier.

His love affair with Astle is different. "He was my first idol," Mainwaring said. "I idolised him more than anybody, and when he died last January, a part of me went with him. It's as deep and important as that."

He has now poured his heart out in tribute to the Albion and England centre-forward in a song he has written with partner Steve Wilson. "Mainwaring and Wilson," he joked, breaking the tension. "It sounds like something out of *Dad's Army*." The song, *Astle is King*, was completed at the weekend - I was given a sneak preview. It goes like this:

With a grace so rare, he'd take to the air,
like a blue and white butterfly.
And he'd weave his way, and seize the day against
the greatest of teams gone by.

BRUM'S THE WORD

And with respect, for our dear Jeff, a song for us all I bring.
Memories prevail, so let us hail for we know
we'll always sing...
Astle is King.

"I started watching him in the late 1960s when the old Smethwick End at The Hawthorns resembled a cow shed. He was just fantastic," Mainwaring said. "The song is my way of doing a bit to help the Astle Memorial Fund and keep the great man's name alive. It's a song right out of my heart for him - the club's one and only King. Who knows? I could have a Christmas number one on my hands," he added.

The run-up to Christmas is a busy time for Mainwaring. He's currently working on the music for Beverley Callard's keep fit video; "You know the one, she played Liz MacDonald in Coronation Street," he said. Then there's a gig this weekend at the Robin Hood pub in Brierley Hill where he will take centre stage as lead singer of his David Bowie tribute band *Jean Genie*. He is Bowie again at the Flowerpot Club in Derby and the Limelight Club in Crewe next month, and then he flies off to tour Bangkok in December - a country still barmy about the *Spiders From Mars*. Next year, he's booked for a Bowie tour of Belgium.

His passion for Bowie began in 1972. These days, when Mainwaring puts on the make-up and dons the gear, he is the spitting image of his hero. "I saw him singing *Starman* on 'Top of the Pops' and that was it," he said. "I loved his voice, started buying the albums and gradually began to copy him. In the end I decided to go for it professionally. I auditioned a band, got the costumes made - and the next thing I knew, we were on Breakfast Television with Lorraine Kelly.

"*Jean Genie* was one of Britain's first tribute bands along with the Bootleg Beatles and Bjorn Again - thankfully, we're still going strong. It's all gone exceedingly well."

BRUM'S THE WORD

Whilst impersonating Bowie, Mainwaring first met Aldrin, the American astronaut who, in 1969, famously followed Neil Armstrong out of Apollo XI and onto the surface of the moon. The two have become great friends.

"I was asked to perform *Space Oddity* and *Life on Mars* at the London premier of the Tom Hanks film, *Apollo 13*. Buzz was there and he loved the band. Afterwards, we had an in-depth discussion about UFOs. We seemed to hit it off immediately, and we've kept in touch ever since," he said. "It's one of my great claims to fame."

Mainwaring hopes his Larry Grayson play, *Shut that Door*, will be complete within a couple of years. "Nobody has paid tribute to his life before, but he was such a fascinating and much loved entertainer. I could talk to you about him all day," he said.

His real love, however, lies at The Hawthorns. From next week, the *Astle is King* single will be available from the club shop. Mainwaring is hoping that it does well to help swell funds to build "The Astle Gates" at the ground - a lasting memorial to The King. "If the Albion fans adopt the song as an anthem, that will be a bonus. But I just want to keep the great man's memory alive in the hearts of everybody," he said.

He sighs for a split second, then softly begins to sing.

The sun went down over Smethwick town,
and the bird on the branch won't sing.
On a Netherton Bridge I stand and think,
of when I was just a kid.
...And Astle was King.

Baggies life gets better by degrees for Batson

Saturday, October 5, 2002.

IT IS JUST BEFORE 7.30am. Although it's bright, there is a chill in the air. You can sense that the season is starting to change. It's a crisp morning, reeking of autumn - the type of day that makes you feel prematurely Christmassy, although you are not really sure why.

A security guard, decked out in shades, Elvis quiff and blue bomber jacket, is holding the fort in the foyer of West Bromwich Albion's newly built East Stand "The receptionist doesn't get here until nine," he said. But upstairs, in a cramped open-plan office, it's a hive of activity. This is not an impressive workplace - it's far too higgledy piggledy. But you can tell that it's a place where things get done. Jeremy Peace, the club chairman, and Mike O'Leary, the chief executive, are huddled over a desk in the corner, trying to blot out the hustle and bustle around them. Brendon Batson MBE, Albion's new managing director, is switched on and itching to get stuck in. He's got the contracts of Derek McInnes, the Baggies captain and Andrew Johnson, the midfield player, on his desk. Only the finishing touches remain. It's a big, big Wednesday.

"We're all early starters," Batson laughed, leading me into the boardroom for a bit of peace and quiet. "There just aren't enough hours in the day, but it's very exciting. We're all working extremely hard, giving it our best shot," he added. Albion is home for him and he is loving every minute of life in the Premiership. Enthusiasm oozes from every sinew.

BRUM'S THE WORD

It's not surprising. The mood at The Hawthorns at the moment is reminiscent of the days when Batson was a player. He was Ron Atkinson's first signing in 1978. A snip at £30,000 from Cambridge United. "That was the best move of my life," he said. "The atmosphere at the club was the same then as it is now. We couldn't get to the ground quick enough and Ron was fantastic. He was a fan as well as a manager, but his philosophy was so simple. He used to tell us: 'If it's on the ground - kick it. If it's in the air - head it!'" It was a theory that got Albion into Europe, and within sniffing distance of major honours.

Honest endeavour helped to make Batson a regular in that team and turned him into one of the most respected right backs in the country. When you drink in the full Batson story, though, the fact that he's spent every working day of his life in football is quite remarkable. He came to England from Trinidad at the age of nine with his brother, Godfrey. He was a stranger in a strange place, growing up "as part of the only black family in Tilbury". He'd never seen a football, let alone kicked one. After his first school match, the sports master urged him to take up cricket. Unperturbed, he got involved with a crowd of football-crazy lads and started playing the game morning, noon and night.

"In the end football came naturally to me," Batson said. "If I'd have made friends with the school chess players, I would have ended up playing chess. I was just in the right place at the right time. It's the same with my current job. I had been at the PFA (Professional Footballers' Association) for 18 years and I couldn't think of any reason I'd ever leave. Then this opportunity came along. It's my dream job."

He's swapped the football field for the phone and the e-mail has replaced the euphoria. Instead of dealing with the occasional tricky left flanker, he's now sparring with a glut of just as tricky football agents. One of them is Cyrille Regis, his old Albion team-mate. The pair of them were on opposite sides of the desk recently when they bashed out the details of a new four-year contract for one of Cyrille's players - his nephew Jason Roberts, the Albion striker.

Roberts certainly won't have to endure the racial taunts that both Batson and Regis suffered in those early days. It's something the Albion managing director will never forget. "We had to break down all the barriers," Batson said. "There were no role models for us. Parents of black youngsters didn't want their lads to become professional footballers because they didn't see it as a career for them. We had trouble from terraces and, even in the clubs, there was a whispering campaign. We had it all - black players didn't like the cold and hadn't got the discipline to train. Basically they thought we were all talent and no temperament. Thankfully, it's a different world today.

"The spotlight fell on us because myself, Cyrille and Laurie Cunningham were three black players together, in a first division side which was doing well on a consistent basis. In the football world we became known as the Three Degrees - but we were better singers!"

After 220 Albion appearances, Batson was forced out of the game through injury. He was so desperately angry that he threw his boots into a dustbin and vowed never to kick a ball again. He's been true to his word. "I still haven't got a pair of football boots in the house," he said. "I haven't kicked a ball now for 14 years."

Not that he'd have any trouble in finding a kickabout pal. Another Albion great, Tony "Bomber" Brown, lives just 12 doors away. But with Batson working all hours and Brown recovering from a hip replacement operation, the prospect of a "three-and-in" knock-up seems a little far-fetched.

Both, however, have remained Baggies fanatics, thrilled by an impressive start to the season, which Batson puts down to the team's organisation. He compares Albion to South Korea, the unexpected yet undeniable darlings of the World Cup.

"They were a perfect example of what organisation can do for you," Batson, who witnessed the tournament first hand, said. "Both myself and Howard Wilkinson agreed they were the best "team" in the competition. Their organisation was fantastic and the manager was very innovative. If "Plan A" wasn't working, he'd get up on the touchline and scream out a few instructions. They'd all look at him and do exactly as they were told - it got them a long way."

If Albion continue to adopt the South Korean way, the halcyon days may carry on - and the fans on the Brummie Road End will have to learn a new chant. It would go something like this: "Fi-ting ka-pang!". Roughly translated, that's South Korean for: "Let's do well handbags". It's the closest you're ever going to get to: "Come on you Baggies".

* *Sheila Ferguson, the original and most famous member of the Three Degrees, sits exhausted in her dressing room at the Birmingham Hippodrome. She's just thrilled another live audience with her performance in the travelling hit musical "Oh! What a Night." She flops into a grotty red plastic chair, in front of a mirror that is surrounded by light bulbs. Two words, however, bring the smile back to her still glamorous face. Suddenly she's got a spring in her step - the memories are flooding back. For a moment she is transformed into the teenager that stepped out onto the stage of the Shea Stadium in the 1960s when her pop group "opened" for the Beatles. ("I was convinced I was going to marry Paul McCartney," she remembers).*

"Cyrille Regis," I enquire innocently. "Ohhhhh," she squeals like a 16-year-old. "He's lovely. Poetry in motion." It's a Paul McCartney moment all over again. Sheila met Cyrille, Brendon Batson and the late Laurie

Cunningham on The Hawthorns pitch before Albion's home match with Everton on April 7, 1979. They had a publicity picture taken - the Three Degrees Sheila, Valerie Holliday and Helen Scott, face to face with Albion's own three degrees.

"That was my first football match," Sheila, who's now bounding around the room full of vigour, said. "After the match Cyrille took me out for a Chinese meal but I had lost my voice through shouting 'Come on you Baggies'. At the end of the evening I just about managed to growl - 'When will I see you again?' It's a good line for a song that, don't you think?"

Sheila went on to hit the headlines thanks to her friendship with the Prince of Wales. "I was introduced to his mother. I didn't know whether to curtsey or bow so in the end, I lunged and stepped on her toe. I gave him street credibility and he ruined my sex life!" she added. "Men wouldn't touch me with a ten-foot barge pole after that. They would all tell me I was Charlie's Angel and therefore, untouchable."

As I say goodnight, I promise faithfully to track down the 1979 picture. She's been trying to get a copy of it for years. "Don't you forget, now," she wails down the corridor as Tom the smiling stage doorkeeper lets me out. "They tell me you're a man of your word. If you fail this time, I'll get a contract out on you and have your kneecaps blown off."

Friday, June 30, 2003

Brendon Batson was sacked as managing director of West Bromwich Albion on Friday, June 20, 2003 following the club's relegation to the Nationwide League first division. Jeremy Peace, the Albion chairman, said: "Regrettably, there will not be a sufficiently meaningful role for Brendon in the future and we have therefore faced up to what is a very difficult decision. He did a great job for us. He is a lovely bloke."

A distraught Batson said: "I didn't join the club to be here for just 12 months. It was my new beginning, but it has been short-lived. Obviously, I'm very disappointed but I have now got to get on with my life."

* Batson's Albion dream was over.

Ding dong, the bells are going to chime

Friday, October 11, 2002.

TREVOR SCOTT is getting married in the morning. He hasn't got much choice.

Scott, a lifelong West Bromwich Albion supporter, made a rash promise to his long-term girlfriend Jane Owen that he would tie the knot once The Baggies had secured promotion to the Premiership and played Liverpool at Anfield. He made his pledge when Gary Megson became the club's manager. Albion were struggling to survive in the first division and things at The Hawthorns were looking bleak.

Megson turned the club's fortunes around, and Scott, from North Springfield in Sedgley, has remained true to his word. Football's very own Romeo and Juliet will be married tomorrow at Dudley Register Office. The date was carefully chosen by the groom - Albion are without a match.

"What else could I do?" Scott said. "I made the promise when it looked as if Albion were going into the second division. Now they've made it into the Premiership, I've got to stay true to my word. I'm a man of honour, Black Country through and through. I was delighted when we went up - but I realised I'd have to go down the aisle. It was all swings and roundabouts."

"It's going to be an Albion wedding," Jane, who works for Dudley Council's housing department, added. "I will be in a white dress and Trevor in a blue suit. The bridesmaids will be in blue and white and we've even got blue and white-stripped confetti.

"My husband-to-be, has insisted that the wedding cake has an Albion crest on the top instead of the traditional bride and groom," she added. "He's such a big Albion fan that we have to have a Baggies calendar above the bed."

"The only fly in the ointment is that the photographer is a Wolves fan," Scott mumbled miserably. "But I do love Jane," he insisted. "Almost as much as I love the Albion."

Driven by an obsession for everything blue

Saturday, October 12, 2002.

CAROLE VERNON, a cleaning lady from Chelmsley Wood, looks miserably out of the window of the black cab. "You lose the will to live travelling with him," she mutters, with a face as long as a fiddle. "All he ever goes on about is football. It does my cowing head in. I might as well talk to the dog."

Driver Paul Collins is taking Carole and her mate, Elaine Gower (who has a son called David), to a job in Pemberton Street, Hockley, in the north west of the city. He's in full flow on his favourite subject - Birmingham City. "I was born on November 23, 1964 ... the same day as Frank Worthington, arguably the most charismatic player we've ever had," he says, carefully moving his beef and Branston pickle sandwiches out of the way of Carole's mop bucket. "But if I could come back as anyone who ever walked the earth, it would have to be Trevor Francis. He is my complete idol."

Paul's cab travels at an average 40 mph. He talks at more than twice that speed. At times he almost hits a high-pitched squeal, such is his enthusiasm for the matter in hand. And the matter in hand is always his beloved Blues. "All right then girls, this is where our journey ends," he says, cheerfully pulling the cab to an abrupt halt outside a faceless office block on the outskirts of the Jewellery Quarter. Carole wrestles with her dustpan and brush, while Elaine awkwardly hauls a long feather duster out onto the pavement. "Paul, you're my little treasure," Elaine says as she wrestles with a large container of industrial bleach. "Up the Villa," she shouts by way of a parting shot.

Paul doesn't mind. He rates the "Enckelman derby" as one of the highlights of his Blues supporting career, and another three points at West Ham United last Saturday has sent him into overdrive. "Next stop St Andrew's," he titters, rubbing his hands in glee. Soon he's thundering down Birmingham's Middle Ring Road in a taxi he bought off a "Brighton fan" eight years ago. It's a short journey. He could do it with his eyes closed, but there's enough time for more than a dozen football stories to tumble randomly from his mouth. It's a unique, scattergun approach, cataloguing the "unofficial" history of Birmingham City Football Club in the minutest detail.

"Seat 168, block ten, row 13. Right behind Enckelman. That's where I worship," he says, giving you a brief introduction. The seats either side are occupied by his sons Jack and Daniel ("It's funny that, I don't even like whiskey"). Paul digresses for a moment. "Our Danny came home once and asked for a Villa shirt because everyone at his school was wearing one. I told him to go and live with his nan. I wasn't going to feed him until he got the idea out of his head. It was as simple as that." A Blues Playoff Winners 2002 pennant swings from his rear view mirror as he proudly points to the newsagent's shop where, one night in 1972, he bought a bag of pear drops before his first game, against Newcastle United.

Past the Highgate mosque and Paul has already described goals from an all-star cast of former Blues players. His descriptions are both passionate and graphic. You can almost see the ball flying in off the boot of Kenny Burns against Norwich in 1974. Before you've caught your breath, Bob Hatton loops one in into the top corner, and finally, his idol Francis almost breaks the back of the net against Carlisle in1975.

Within a flick of his indicator, he's moved on to the present day. Now he's singing the praises of Steve Bruce, the Birmingham manager. The St Andrew's floodlights appear in the distance and he lets out a mini growl of anticipation. "Bruce has done a magnificent job," he says regaining his composure. "I was beginning to think nobody would ever take us out of the football wilderness." Paul thinks for a second. "He's a modern-day Moses, I suppose."

"Do you know," adds the cabbie, moving down a gear to negotiate a tricky island, yet with his mind still racing on, "I've had them all in the back of this cab. Karren Brady, the lot. If ever there was a pick-up from St Andrew's, I'd volunteer to do it. There's only one person I would ever refuse - John Mitchell, the Fulham player whose last-minute goal robbed us of an FA Cup Final at Wembley in 1975. I cried my eyes out. I've never forgiven him."

Arriving at St Andrew's, Paul - who also writes endless poetry on his favourite passion - spins the cab around on an almost deserted car park. But there's no time to ponder. Wearing his uniform of Blues shirt and black training bottoms, he strides gallantly towards the ground telling me of his football "treasure chest" which includes a Subbuteo player that once stood on top of a cake baked to mark Trevor Francis's international debut. He also once brought a crush barrier from the Tilton Road stand before it was demolished (He took it home in the back of his cab before erecting it in the garden of his Kingshurst home) and he's the proud owner of a signed shirt from Roger "Harry" Willis who scored a goal every time Paul drove him to a match.

At the moment, his heroes are Aliou Cisse and Robbie Savage. "If you put Savage's heart under the bonnet of my cab, it would run forever. I'd never need to buy another drop of diesel again," he says. "Cisse and Savage, the best double act since Batman and Robin."

Paul is keen to lead me inside St Andrew's, where a young receptionist looks on in bewilderment. "There's Trevor," he declares, looking at a black and white team photograph from 1973. He goes on to name every player in the picture and how many goals he saw them score.

"I'll sum it up like this," he says on our way back to Edgbaston. "Football is the be all and end all of life". The history lesson is over. The fare is just over £8. The entertainment value has been priceless.

"Even your eyes are Birmingham City blue," I tell him as I leave the cab. "I know," he replies without hesitation. "I had them painted!"

Sunday, October 13, 2002.

Robbie Savage is ordered by Steve Bruce, the Birmingham City manager, to get his hair cut. The pin-up boy of St Andrew's has always been associated with his spectacular blonde-flowing barnet. But Bruce wants the trademark 'Savage shampoo and set' removed, arguing that a short back and sides or, at the very least, a barber's 'trim and tidy' might help to improve his image. "Maybe if he got a haircut, he wouldn't stand out so much," Bruce, concerned at Savage's record of four bookings in six games, said.

THERE'S ONLY ONE ROBBIE SAVAGE
By Paul Collins.
(Chelmsley Wood taxi driver)

Robbie Savage, the maestro, is like no other I've seen.
He gives one hundred per cent for the fans and the team.
What makes him so different is his will and desire.
So misunderstood. I just watch and admire.

BRUM'S THE WORD

The Blues' faithful love him, cause he plays from the heart,
He gives everything he's got - to the end, from the start.
Over exuberant at times, but a cheat - certainly not.
He gets in where it hurts and what bottle he's got.

With the heart of a lion, he hates to get beat.
On the pitch he's a winner, don't mention defeat.
What an engine he has. He's all over the place,
Love him or loathe him, he fills newspaper space.

Robbie's my idol. He's different - it's true.
He's a working class lad. Just like me - and like you.
To call him anything different, is an insult to our game.
Because without players like Robbie, football wouldn't be
the same.

* Robbie Savage was named Birmingham's player of the
year at the end of the season. He remained true to his long
locks. He still has the same hair-style.

Sweet dreams are made of goals for Taylor

Saturday, October 19, 2002.

JAMES ROBERTS, West Bromwich's very own Willy Wonka, grimaces as he tugs up his jacket to avoid a severe soaking. "This," he says, pointing to the heavens as torrential rain batters the Black Country, "is the sugar boiler's worst nightmare."

The downpour has come at the worst possible time. Today they're gearing up for a "royal visitor" at the Sela Traditional Sweet Company Limited, a firm that has been in the Roberts family since 1882, when James's great-grandparents, Arthur and Elizabeth, took over a small kitchen at the back of a shop in Alfred Street. Even the copper sugar boilers that have been with the Roberts clan for more than a century have been given a special rinse. But the damp atmosphere is a curse. It gets into the machines and makes the sweet mixture too sticky.

The visitor isn't really a royal. To fans of West Bromwich Albion, he's far more important than that. It's Bob Taylor, the club's favourite son and Black Country folk hero.

Taylor is celebrating his testimonial this season and the sweet people at Sela have been asked to turn out a new product - Super Bobby's Bon Bons - in time for the derby game with Birmingham City today. By this morning, 800 bags will have been dispatched to The Hawthorns. They'll be snapped up in next to no time.

"They're in the four club colours: blue, white, yellow and green," Roberts says as he welcomes Taylor to the factory, now in Thynne Street. The Albion man is on time. He always is. He's as polite and unassuming as ever as he squeezes into the factory uniform of white coat, hat and light blue over-shoes. He hasn't come to watch the sweets being made - he fully intends to make them himself.

Taylor, who joined the club in January 1992, has become an Albion legend. You only have to surf his testimonial web site - www.super-bob.co.uk - to appreciate the depth of feeling for the man whose 131 goals have taken Albion up, kept them up, and taken them up again. Young fan Ally Ayres summed it up beautifully. "You were the first man I ever called my hero," he wrote on the Taylor message board. "My dad had Jeff Astle, my granddad had Ronnie Allen…but I had you. I will always remember you as the greatest player I saw as a lad." Another Baggies fan has added: "Thank you Super Bob. It's been a privilege to watch you over the years. In a time when our game is being taken over by greed and scandal, you have stayed a credit to yourself and to football. You're a first class, down to earth gentleman - and a true legend."

Taylor, 35, will always be grateful for their support. "I've lived a dream for the last ten years," he says spreading sterilised talc on his grey gloves. An almost overwhelming smell of neat syrup fills the nostrils as John Wilkinson, the chief sugar boiler, keeps his eye on a mixture of sugar and glucose that is simmering away at a temperature of more than 150 degrees centigrade. "It's lovely to know that I've touched people in a certain way," Taylor says.

"But the feeling is mutual. I will always be in debt to the fans for the way they've accepted me. They've taken me to their hearts and that means everything."

Sela employees June and Eileen, who between them have clocked up nearly 20 years in the sweet making trade, are busy shovelling castor sugar into an orange cement mixer on the other side of the factory floor. Taylor re-focuses his mind on the job in hand. "I'm good at this," he says, spreading navy blue colouring onto the molten liquid which now fills a huge silver tray. "I used to be a painter and decorator - it's all in the wrist."

Wilkinson, the master, is not so sure. "You've got to be careful with the blue. If you get it wrong it comes out turquoise!" he says scooping a dollop of treacle-like liquid onto his spatula for inspection. He should know. Under his watchful eye, the company turns out thousands of humbugs, bon bons, fizzballs, bulls-eyes and Sela Cough Sweets - probably their most famous line.

Thankfully, the mixture that Taylor is working on, turns out "true Baggie blue" giving him time to turn his attention back to football. "It's my one remaining wish to score a Premiership goal for Albion," he says peering at a newly made batch of barley sugars. "It's a dream if you like. I just love the club." It might come today if he can shake off an irritating Achilles injury.

"I've got a good record against Blues," he said. "I've scored in nearly every game I've played against them. But it's a funny fixture. The rivalry between the fans is not as intense as an Albion versus Wolves game, or Blues versus Villa. It's the gentle derby. I think the supporters have a sort of admiration for each other - probably because they've had their fair share of suffering." Under instruction, Taylor has started to fold a "soft centre" into his sweet mixture. It's not a difficult job for him. "I used to watch my mum do this when she was making pies," he says, remembering his youth in the North East town of Horden. He began his football life as a centre half until the games master at his school, Dean House Comprehensive, moved him up front. The goals soon started to flow.

After a spell at Horden Colliery Welfare, Billy Bremner gave Taylor his first professional contract, at Leeds United. Before long he moved to Bristol City and then came the first of two Albion spells, interrupted briefly by a season or two in the Premiership with Bolton Wanderers.

"Like most of the fans," he says carefully avoiding two crushed humbugs on the factory floor, "I didn't think Albion would ever be back in the top flight. I've lived for this. It's unreal." He stares at a bath containing half a ton of sugar as his bon bons make their way to June and Eileen's vibrating wrapping machine. "But we've seen nothing we're frightened of yet. I honestly think Albion and Blues will stay up. If you've got the right spirit you're half way there - and team spirit is our greatest strength."

Before long the sweets - blackcurrant blue, lemon white, lime green and pineapple yellow - are ready and packed. The label shows Taylor celebrating his goal against Crystal Palace, the one that secured Albion promotion last season. He asks if he can have a copy of the picture blown up for his wall. "It's another golden memory. I've got them all stored up in here," he says pointing to his forehead.

If that forehead can head home just one more goal - Bob Taylor's Albion story will be complete.

* Bob Taylor never scored his "dream goal" in the Premiership. He was never really given a chance. After four starts on the bench at the beginning of the season, Gary Megson, the Albion manager, refused to include him in his first team squad. He was banished. Forced to train with the club's youngsters - he maintains he was never given a reason. Taylor did start the last game of the season against Newcastle - his farewell appearance. Unfortunately he hobbled out of the action with an injury after 31 minutes. He was given a magnificent standing ovation.

His testimonial game against a Bryan Robson Select team on Tuesday, May 13, was attended by more than

16,000 supporters. In an emotional speech after the match, he told supporters: "Next season, I will be a fan - just like the rest of you." His loyalty to the club was even mentioned on the floor of the House of Commons. West Bromwich West MP, Adrian Bailey, tabled a Commons motion heralding the forward's "outstanding contribution to football". The Labour MP said Taylor's loyalty and sportsmanship deserved "the respect and admiration of everyone who loves football."

Bob Taylor remains a Hawthorns legend.

Ballet who?

DION DUBLIN has the sharp-eyed stare of a true marksman. His hunger and temperament is that of a winner. When he removes his training top, he has the body of a finely tuned athlete. Yet when the Aston Villa striker steps out of the football spotlight, he immerses himself in the fantasy world of *The Nutcracker*. He's enchanted by the romance of *Romeo and Juliet*. He marvels at the elegance of *Swan Lake*. Football may be his first love, but ballet is his passion - his lifeline.

The 33-year-old was smitten by the ballet bug three years ago. It was December 1999 and he was recovering from a fractured neck vertebra, sustained in a collision with Gerald Sibon, of Sheffield Wednesday. For a time, there were fears that he might have to spend the rest of his life in a wheelchair. That Christmas, he and his wife, Louise, went to the Birmingham Royal Ballet's (BRB) production of *The Nutcracker* at the city's Hippodrome Theatre. By the end of the first act, he was well and truly hooked. He'd found an artistic soul mate.

"I remember the interval," Dublin said. "I was so excited that I couldn't wait to go and discuss the storyline. I thought to myself, blimey! I'm really into this. I was desperate to go back in and see what happened next. Since then, ballet's become my release. It's good to go, switch off and enjoy the whole experience. In a way, I go into the fantasy world of the piece. I imagine I'm in their fairytale land. I'm up there with them."

In his world, a ballet lover can often be seen as an oddball, but Dublin is different. With refreshing honesty he's determined to help break down the snobbery and the sniggering that still surrounds the world of ballet. But even he admits it's an uphill challenge trying to persuade his Villa team-mates to swap their free kicks and corners for pirouettes and *pas de deux*.

"I'm pretty sure none of them have ever been," he said. "They ask me, 'what are you going to the theatre for?' I tell them to go to a ballet they may have heard of and have a look. I know if they go to the BRB once, they'll go back. I'm trying to get them there, I really am." He ponders for a minute. Dublin is a man who thinks hard about every word he says, yet he's confident in his delivery. "At least they can't give me any stick if they haven't tried it themselves." He thinks again. "To be honest, I don't care what they think. I know I'm on to a good thing."

Dublin was given the chance to perform on a different stage last year when the artistic director and choreographer of the Birmingham Royal Ballet, David Bintley (an Aston Villa season ticket holder), asked him to perform in a one-off charity show called "The Cracked Nut".

"I was tempted," Dublin said. "David Bintley is a top man. But the performance clashed with a match so I was unable to take part. I'd certainly think about it if I were offered the chance again. I'd do anything for the BRB, they're just all so normal, no airs and graces. They've taught me that ballet is for everyone. You don't have to be a connoisseur or wear a dinner jacket. I admire the way they are trying to open the art out so that it touches the people - all people. I think they deserve all the support in the world."

His praise of the BRB is a constant theme as we chat in the players' lounge at Aston Villa's Bodymoor Heath training ground. As far as Dublin's concerned, he's a ballet buff and proud of it. But a normal one! He's also an eloquent orator, the thinking man's footballer. He listens to Classic FM on the way to training, and, when he's not playing the beautiful game or watching the beautiful art, he's making beautiful music on his saxophone.

Although he's adamant that football will always be his first love, he's become such a regular at the Hippodrome that he and his wife have become Friends of the BRB. Membership of that organisation has given him a unique insight into the world of the ballet dancer. A world that never ceases to enthral him.

"I was invited to the Hippodrome to see the ballet dancers train," he said. "Their dedication and commitment is unbelievable, amazing. They never stop working. It made me think that football must be the laziest profession of them all. I would guarantee it is!" He thinks for a minute. "And they all talk to you. In my experience with football, you wouldn't expect a star of the game to go and discuss his performance with a spectator straight afterwards. You have to fight your way into my world. With ballet dancers, they are more than happy to talk about a show once they've come off the stage. They're more on your level." A hint of passion mixed with a tinge of frustration creeps into his voice. "But people don't know that because they don't go. They have their own set views on ballet and the theatre in general. But if they don't go, how will they ever know."

Dublin's proudest ballet possession is a signed pair of point shoes from Molly Smolen, the American who is one of his favourite principal dancers. They were actually given to his wife as a birthday present and now they hang in the Dublins' kitchen, dwarfed by the footballer's size 12 boots that make them look like a pair of baby's booties. His favourite productions are *Swan Lake* and Sir Peter Wright's version of *The Nutcracker*, which is still performed annually at the Birmingham Hippodrome.

As Dublin has become more technically aware, he has started to appreciate the work and art of a principal ballerina more and more: "I do tend to watch the principals really closely. I like to see how they hold their hands and position their feet. I know what I like in a ballet and I'm quite good with timing. That's something you pick up from football, or in my case, football and my music. Yeh!" He looks straight ahead. "I suppose I'm really getting into it!"

As is his family. Louise is a former dancer and even Claudia, his five-year-old daughter, has recently started ballet lessons three times a week at a school near the family home in Stratford-Upon-Avon. She'll attend her first professional production with mum and dad before too long.

On the field, Dublin is enjoying a resurgence this season having wrestled his way back into the team ahead of Marcus Allback and Peter Crouch, manager Graham Taylor's costly summer arrivals. He puts his newly found lease of life down to sheer hard work.

"I've just got my head down and got on with my job," he said. "The gaffer didn't want to use me at the start of the season and you can't really blame him. He brought new players to the club and had to put them in. But I kept myself fit and I do think you get rewarded if you work hard. I like to work hard. I like to think I've earned what I've got. I started my football career in non-league, working in ice cream factories and leisure centres to make ends meet. I know what I've got and I've worked hard for it."

The youngest of three brothers growing up in Leicester, Dublin was so determined to become a professional footballer that any early artistic bent he may have had was quickly put on the back burner. His professional career began with John Beck at Cambridge United in the late 1980s. He soon captured the headlines and his goal scoring exploits took him to Manchester United and then on to Coventry City where he scored 71 goals in 171 appearances. John Gregory brought him to Villa in 1998 for a fee of £5.75 million. He began his Villa career with a dramatic burst of goals, but injuries have set him back. Having fought his way into the limelight again, he's now in hot pursuit of one more Premiership goal to take him to the 100 mark.

Two goals against Luton Town in the recent Worthington Cup tie may have bought him more time to achieve that milestone. But, after the game, there was no time for Dublin to celebrate. He had a more pressing engagement across the city. The match clashed with the opening night of *Concert Fantasy*, Bintley's latest work, a classical ballet set to the music of Tchaikovsky. Knowing how important a successful opening night was to the company, Dublin raced to the Hippodrome to see how the production had gone and what the reaction had been.

It's part of his simple, yet unstintingly loyal way of paying back the Birmingham Royal Ballet, an organisation that has helped broaden his horizons, that has, in no small way, enriched his life. Dion Dublin is like that.

* Dion Dublin scored his 100th Premiership goal in the 71st minute of Villa's 4-1 home win over West Ham United in November.

On March 3, however, the elegant and eloquent thinking man's footballer, appeared to lose his mind when he was sent off for head-butting midfielder Robbie Savage during Villa's explosive local derby match with Birmingham City at Villa Park. Dublin was forced to apologise to his team-mates at a hastily arranged press conference the following day.

"I have never done anything like that in my career before. I'm ashamed of what I have done," he said. "I've let the players, the manager and the staff down - and most importantly I have let myself down. I called a meeting of my team-mates this morning and said sorry to them. I wanted to say sorry to their faces."

Dublin, who bellowed the word "cheat" directly at a television camera as he left the field, was given an automatic three match ban and later fined £6,000 by the Football Association for "improper conduct".

Why Birmingham City didn't have a prayer

Saturday, October 26, 2002.

"THE LORD GIVETH and the Lord taketh away. Blessed be the name of the Lord" [Job1:21]. Today, I will be preaching from the ancient book of football derby matches. In other words, let me explain how West Bromwich Albion and Birmingham City shared a point apiece at The Hawthorns last weekend.

The story centres around Darren Moore, the mountainous Albion central defender. A born-again Christian, Moore spent the evening before the big game spreading the word of God before a congregation of 180 at Carters Lane Baptist Church in Halesowen.

It was a wonderful experience - you could sense it was going to be. At the entrance to the church a full-size cardboard cut-out of the six-foot two-inch 16stone defender stood next to a poster of a yacht struggling to negotiate a stormy sea. The caption below read: "He whom God steers, sails safely". Inside, a video of Albion's promotion season was being played on a projector screen at the altar, beneath a stained glass window depicting Jesus with hands outstretched. The congregation, many wearing Baggies shirts, crammed themselves into the pews. The purple *Revised English Bibles*, piled at the end of each row, were not needed tonight. Instead, those gathered, encouraged by their host for the evening, stood as one - and then began to "boing, boing" in expectation of the imminent arrival of their hero. This was worship at its very best.

"I became a Christian in a hairdresser's shop in Causeway Green," one of the dearly beloved told me. "I'm a season-ticket holder in the East Stand," he added, proudly, pointing to the back of his young nephew's shirt. A large red number 5 was encircled by the words "Big Dave". It's the defender's nickname, which he gets because he resembles the actor in the Pot Noodle adverts.

Moore turned up early for the occasion and was instantly at ease. The church is home for him. It's just as much his territory as the six-yard box is during a game. He told the congregation: "The Lord loves you, it doesn't matter which walk of life you come from. When I play football, He knows I'll be competing to win. But when I come off the field, I give thanks to Him - win, lose or draw - for giving me the strength to have got through another match."

Less than nine hours later, Moore, who has been a revelation for Albion in the Premiership this season, bizarrely put the ball into his own net to give Birmingham City the lead in that second-city derby. The Lord, it seemed, had just taken away. Moore held out his hands in desperation before grabbing the ball from the back of the net and tearing back to the centre circle to re-start play. Perhaps he could sense that, true to his word, the Lord was also about to giveth.

And He did. Ninety seconds later, Jason Roberts snatched a late equaliser. The first player to congratulate him was Moore, who ran fully 40 yards to embrace his team-mate. For a second, the two came together. What they said to each other may never be known, but if you'd have been at Carters Lane Baptist Church the night before, you might have had a good idea. Moore explained: "I have a fellow Christian at the club - Jason Roberts. He asked me to share the Lord with him and as a result, he's asked the Lord into his life."

Roberts and Moore, two footballers strong enough to stand up for their faith and revel in the joy it brings them, had played the decisive roles in one of the region's biggest games of the season - within the space of a minute and a half. After the equaliser, Baggie Bird, the Albion mascot, threw his wings to the heavens as the crowd behind him in the Birmingham Road End sang the club's adopted anthem - Psalm 23. "The Lord's my Shepherd I'll not want - he makes me down to lie".

At Carters Lane Baptist Church the night before, there was no singing. The hymn board was blank, but the questions to Moore flowed thick and fast. "What happened to Wolves' 12-point lead over Albion last season?" asked a lone Wolverhampton Wanderers fan in the audience. A young man next to me inquired: "Have you prayed for any of the referees after matches this season?" Moore was non-committal.

The Rev Minister Andrew Millns, a self-confessed Manchester City nut, darted in and out of the aisles, handing out yellow leaflets to let the congregation know more about his beloved 60-year-old place of worship, which sits in the heart of the Black Country and is tastefully decorated in Baggies navy blue and white. He'd had a busy week. The Ladies' Circle meeting on Tuesday, Boys' Brigade on Thursday, and now this - his biggest congregation for many weeks.

Moore was a delight. Answering honestly questions on racism, his love for the game that began at the age of 8, his love for Aston Villa as a teenager growing up in Handsworth, his new love for West Bromwich Albion, and, of course, his unstinting love for the Lord - a relationship that began when he witnessed first hand the power of prayer, which helped his then Bradford City team-mate, Wayne Jacobs, overcome a career threatening knee injury. "We prayed for Wayne's knee and the Lord healed it," he said.

Outside the church, the illuminated clock read 8.47pm. The Wolves fan looked quizzically at Church deacon Helen Plimmer, another Albion season-ticket holder who was balancing delicately on her crutches after an ankle operation. "I still can't understand about the 12 points!" the Wolves fan stressed.

Helen shrugged her shoulders. "Maybe it was the work of the Lord," she answered before hobbling off to the church hall for a well-deserved complimentary cup of coffee.

The Lord, it seems, works in mysterious ways - His wonders to perform.

Darren Moore's season came to an abrupt and premature end when he was stretchered off the field during Albion's home match against Chelsea on Sunday, March 16. Moore clashed with Jimmy Floyd Hasselbaink after 15 minutes of the game, which Albion lost 2-0. He underwent a successful knee ligament operation the following month, but missed his side's remaining eight fixtures.

Butler still serving up treats on the airwaves

Saturday, November 2, 2002.

TONY BUTLER doesn't burst into a room - he explodes. The man who invented the football phone-in still has the youthful exuberance of one of the greyhounds that used to race for him around Hall Green dog track.

At 67, he cuts a dashing figure. Standing as straight as a gun barrel, he struts around like a peacock. The collars of his immaculate black polo shirt stand bolt upright, brushing against his trademark neatly trimmed, yet greying beard and moustache. There is a small silver microphone pinned to the lapel of his shocking mauve jacket (always dapper, he boasts: "I've got enough clothes in my wardrobe to last until I'm 110"). He's a mentor to some, a legend to many and a broadcasting giant to all.

It's Monday evening, and Butler is preparing for his weekly show on BBC WM. Although now semi-retired, he still lives for football, although he combines his weekly radio stint with another job - doorman at his wife's dance club at St Dominic's church hall in Staffordshire. "It costs them £2.50 an hour and I'm the bouncer," he growled in that familiar West Midlands accent. Butler doesn't dance himself. "I'm a perpetual beginner," he said. "When the others have moved up, I stay in the beginners' class so that I will look a bit better than the rest." He smiles. A memory has stirred in his ever-active brain. "But I did once win £500 in a tango competition," he added proudly.

Butler, the son of a farmer, has a mind for detail. He remembers his early years vividly. "We had 24 acres in Lower Penn," he said with a tongue still as sharp as a tack. At Wolverhampton Grammar School he was "useless - not interested". But he showed promise editing the school magazine and was still a pupil when he became a part-time sports journalist for a Wolverhampton news agency. His first job was to cover a rugby match and football game at the same time while sheltering under an oak tree that separated the two pitches. It was a baptism of fire - the Butler story had begun.

After a spell as office boy at the *Birmingham Post and Mail* and then as a freelance rugby writer, his life took a dramatic twist in 1973 when he applied for a job on BRMB, a new commercial radio station for Birmingham. "I met a man called Keith Hayes who came from Vancouver to organise the station," Butler recalled. "He asked me what I would do if I became BRMB's sports editor. I told him I'd introduce a phone-in for the fans. We shook hands and I went home thinking I'd shot myself in the foot. I'd had the idea, and got the job - but I hadn't got a clue how it was going to work." That handshake changed the face of British broadcasting forever.

"The phone-in was unheard of in those days," Butler said. "But we were stunned at the reaction. I remember my first night. I got 28 calls. Within a matter of months, we were flying."

Over the next decade, Butler became a Birmingham institution. He introduced the infamous "prayer mat" for West Bromwich Albion and Aston Villa fans during their epic European adventures. Listeners were urged to go "on their knees" in an effort to conjure a goal. He was banned from nearly every ground in the Midlands for his straight talking - and was immortalised in a sketch by comedian Jasper Carrott, who used to play in Butler's charity football team. ("I was the self appointed chairman. It meant I could sack the manager if we had a bad game.")

Carrott's routine focussed on an exasperated reporter who, thwarted in his bid to get an interview with John Osborne, the West Brom goalkeeper, after a promotion winning match at Oldham in 1976, declared to a live and expectant wireless audience: "He's p****d off, Tone!" Butler recalled: "The reaction to that television show was unbelievable. I had phone calls from all over the country until 4am, then I rang Jasper and threatened to sue him for £1 million."

After ten and a half years, Butler was unceremoniously dumped by BRMB after a very public fracas with a colleague. The memory still upsets him today. "I thought I'd never work again," he said. "But, after being sacked on the Monday, I was back at work for the BBC by Wednesday, to everyone's complete and utter amazement."

The sacking, though, wasn't his greatest disappointment. That came at Hall Green greyhound stadium, when his dog, Farmer Brown, came third in the prestigious BBC TV Trophy having led around the last bend. "I was gutted," Butler confessed. "I thought I was going to win but the dog faded a couple of yards from the line." He looks down for a second and shakes his head. "It was the biggest upset of my whole career."

Suddenly, Butler bolts out of his chair. His show is about to start. He's done thousands over the years, but tonight there's an edge to the man. He's just come out of hospital after an operation to remove a blockage from his stomach. He collapsed two weeks ago after coming home from his local. For a moment he thought he was going to die. "I was scared stiff. That's the truth," he said, entering Studio Four at Pebble Mill. It's 6.55pm and he's due on air in five minutes. Work has always been his great passion. It's what turns him on. What makes him tick "The doctor told me to take four weeks off," he said. "I told him to get on his bike." (It's Butler's catchphrase).

He reflects for a second. "Do you know," he said quietly. "I don't think I'll ever retire - I don't quite know what I would do.

I've never been one for sitting around." The voice that has sacked a thousand managers has developed a slight tinge of emotion. It doesn't last long. A red light shines in his studio. The microphone is live and Butler the gentleman is immediately transformed. He's now a performer and when Butler performs, he's still the best in the business.

"Tonight we're taking no prisoners. Kick down the doors," he encourages his audience. He taunts listeners, suggesting Graham Taylor, the Villa manager, has lost the plot. "Him and Doug Ellis deserve each other. They should be married - but don't ask me to give either of them away," he barks. "I told you Albion wouldn't win six games all season," he roars in his next breath. "Give me a call and we'll kick it around."

The lines are open. For the next three hours, Tony Butler is in command of the airwaves. He wouldn't have it any other way.

* BBC Five Live's David Law, via email, writes: "I'm sitting on the centre court at the Paris tennis tournament preparing to broadcast on the likes of Marat Safin and Carlos Moya. I've just read your story on Tony Butler. Fantastic memories, and for me, someone who's just had his first taste of broadcasting this year as part of the BBC Five Live Wimbledon tennis team, a great inspiration."

* Adrian Williams, via email, writes: "I was reading the brilliant Butler article on the Tube and started laughing out loud (caused a few raised eyebrows on the Jubilee Line). I remember the prayer mats very well. Murray Walker and co should be praying at the alter of Tony Butler. He should have been a national institution.

* Tony Butler still enjoys a cult following for his weekly football phone-ins on BBC WM.

Oggie, Oggie, Oggie…

Tuesday, November 5, 2002.

OGGIE WHITEHEAD, Aston Villa fanatic and prolific non-league striker, stares at the antique pine sideboard in his Warwickshire lounge. He looks longingly at his discarded wedding ring that sits awkwardly next to an overdue gas bill and various collectable trinkets. The ring serves as a dramatic reminder of his luckless start to the football season.

Oggie, who plays for Nuneaton Griff in the Midland Football Combination Premier Division, shakes his head in despair. He's one of the game's unfortunate casualties. He has been sidelined after two freak collisions with the same goalpost. He's lost his place in the team - and one of his fingers.

The forward's tale of woe began when he was forced out of the game due to a minor injury in September. To aid his recovery, and get him back among the goals as soon as possible, Nuneaton Griff allowed Oggie to play "on-loan" for his village team Bourton and Franklin. "That's where the trouble started," he said.

Oggie, who works for Land Rover in Gayden, explained: "I was nobbled by the same goalpost - twice. The first time, I was taking the nets down after my comeback match with Bourton. I jumped to unhinge the corner of the net and, on my way down, I ripped my leg open on one of the goalpost hooks."

The Warwickshire marksman needed 16 stitches to repair the wound. Things were looking bleak - they were about to get worse.

"Before my next comeback game I volunteered for net duty again, at the same end of the ground. In hindsight, I should have learnt my lesson," he said. Sure enough, the dreaded goalpost curse was about to strike again. "As I jumped up to attach the net to the top of the crossbar, I caught my wedding ring on the hook. As I fell to the ground, I looked up to see the ring spinning around on the hook and my finger lying behind me on the pitch. The same goalpost had taken the third finger of my left hand clean off."

Oggie picked up his wedding ring first - then his finger. He walked back to the dressing room where team-mates packed it in ice before packing him off to the local accident hospital. Unfortunately, the digit was too badly damaged to be sewn back on. That's why the ring now sits on the sideboard. It's currently without a finger to sit on.

The injury, meanwhile, left Oggie without a leg to stand on. "I've vowed never to go near a goal-net again," he said. "Unless, of course, it's to put the ball into the back of it."

* Oggie Whitehead returned to the Nuneaton Griff side in February. He went on to score eight goals in 14 games, including a hat-trick against Cheslyn Hay. Griff finished 12th in the Midland Combination Premier Division.

Malcolm Boyden contemplates
in Victoria Square, Birmingham.

Above: Bintley calls the Royal Ballet's programme his "Fixture list".
Below: Albion's "Three Degrees" - from left, Cunningham, Batson and Regis - get to grips with the Seventies' real things.

Above: True Blue: after 30 years of supporting City, Collins remains convinced that "football is the be-all and end-all of life".
Below: Enjoying a jar or two: Albion Supporters have a soft centre as far as Taylor, their legendary goalscorer, is concerned.

Above: Dancing brave: Dublin's love of the ballet may earn him the odd hoot from fans, but he remains a staunch supporter of the art.
Below: Hall mark: Mortimer enjoys an evening's bingo 20 years after lifting the European Cup.

Lazaridis: twin talents.

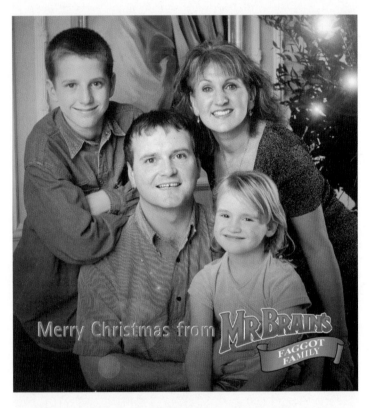

Food for thought: the Doody family
love faggots and Albion.

Aliou Cisse with Birmingham City manager Steve Bruce.

History man: Watts is a loyal and trusted Villa supporter.

"I knew in my heart that football had killed Jeff, but this was the proof." *Laraine Astle*.

From keeping goal to looking after graves: Nearly three decades after hanging up his gloves, Latchford can be found on patrol in cemeteries around Solihull.

Edwards is retiring after almost 30 years
with Moseley.

Jim Lewis: the Agony and the Ecstasy.

Playing by numbers: Rosie Gold, left,
and Thelma Sullivan.

Tindall: unruffled by being physically
attacked and spat at.

"I'm not alone. All around I see hope fading. You ask any football fan. A life without hope is a life not worth living." *Professor Carl Chinn..*

Elvis Music, who once watched Serb soldiers burn his house down, says there were no winners in the Bosnian conflict.

"There were six kids at home. We had nothing.
My Dad could cut a Swiss roll into four hundred slices."
Tom Ross, Capital Gold radio host.

Jack of all trades: Brown retains
his competitive streak.

"If you always look on the dark side of life,
occasionally you'll be pleasantly surprised."
Stuart Rogers, theatre executive director.

Kennedy plays a rhapsody in claret and blue

Saturday, November 9, 2002.

WHEN NIGEL KENNEDY performs, the world listens. He doesn't just play the violin - he makes love to it. Lost in his own never-never land, he caresses the instrument, eyes shut tight. Sparky used to plead with his piano to make magic. Kennedy does the same with his violin, often starring at it madly - demanding perfection.

This is music from the heart, although today his heart is somewhere else - you can tell, because he's got his odd socks on. He may be a musical genius, but Kennedy's real passion is Aston Villa and the socks are one of his football superstitions.

"On match days I have to do things right, man," he said. "The odd socks are all part of it - they keep things going for me. The claret sock goes on the right foot and the blue on the left." Kennedy ponders for a moment, then smiles: "I also drink tea out of my two Villa mugs. They're my match mugs, the same ones every time. It's my pre-match routine," he bows his head. In an instant his mood has changed. There's an air of gloom about the maestro. "It didn't work when we played the Blues though, did it?" he mumbled dejectedly.

Villa blood runs through every vein in Kennedy's body. On the sleeve of his *Greatest Hits* album he has claret and blue war paint smeared across his cheeks. "It's because you have to show your colours," the world's original "punk violinist", who insisted on wearing his Villa scarf when he was featured on *This is Your Life*, said. He's already obtained permission from the club to have his ashes scattered on the Villa Park pitch. "I'm delighted. They very rarely agree, but I'm booked in." He also wrote a song for Paul McGrath, the former Villa defender, entitled: *I Believe In God*. "It's still one of my favourite tunes," he said. "I composed it for him and taped the Villa fans singing about him to put on the recording." He suddenly thrusts his two arms in the air and chants: "Ohh, Ahh Paul McGrath," by way of a demonstration.

Kennedy's Villa story began when he was 7. After moving from Brighton to Birmingham, he was taken to watch the team play Charlton Athletic at Villa Park. It is still a special memory. "Tommy Docherty had just taken over and the atmosphere was remarkable, I was hooked straight away," he said.

His greatest Villa moment, though, came in December 1970. He recalls the game in a flash, then describes almost every kick: "We beat Manchester United in the semi-final of the League Cup with Andy Lochhead and Pat McMahon scoring the goals. United had the world's best - Bobby Charlton, George Best, the lot. I'll never forget it."

Kennedy's six-year-old son, Sark, "an attacking midfielder who tends to model himself on David Beckham", is also bitten by the Villa bug. He went to his first game when he was a toddler. "I told him if he didn't support the Villa he would have to pay the rent."

Sark also shows musical promise. "He loves the energy of music," said Kennedy. "He's into Ian Dury and the Blockheads at the moment and he's desperate for his first electric guitar. He likes the violin because he can strut around pretending to be a pop star like his dad does, but it's the idea of a guitar that he's really fallen in love with. I've told him if he learns piano for a year he can have one."

As a boy sitting under his mother's piano, Kennedy senior first got a feel for music. He later fell under the spell and guidance of Yehudi Menuhin who became a father figure.

Menuhin and Stephane Grappelli shaped Kennedy's early life - and thus helped reshape classical music forever.

"Yehudi was my mentor. He opened my mind to music and taught me to put my heart into it. I still believe music is a communication of the heart," Kennedy said. "Grappelli gave me so much, too. I had two great examples to follow, but they were such extreme, strong characters. It made me realise that everyone should put their own fingerprint on their work and not conform. We're all different and that's something we should celebrate."

A staunch non-conformist, Kennedy, whose 1989 version of Vivaldi's *Four Seasons* sold more than two million copies worldwide, practices for three hours every day. He still loves the "electrical excitement" of live performances, but he never listens to his own recordings. "It's like hearing your voice on an answerphone," he said "When I listen, I think, I can do better than that cat Nigel Kennedy." He treats his priceless Italian-made violin, which dates from 1735, like a child. He has to know where it is every moment of the day and makes sure it's always housed in a climatically controlled environment.

I asked him to name the two greatest influences in his life, convinced I would hear the names Menuhin and Grappelli again. Before I could finish the question, Kennedy announced: "Ron Saunders and Doug Ellis." He refuses to jump onto the "Ellis Out" bandwagon. The Villa chairman, he believes, has done a great job keeping the club out of debt. "Although we need to return to being a great team again," he conceded. "Finishing seventh in the league and getting into the Uefa Cup is not good enough any more." Saunders he rates as "the best manager the West Midlands has ever seen".

The former Villa manager celebrates his 70th birthday today, but unlike Kennedy, he won't spend the morning going through his pre-match rituals. Saunders refuses to talk football to anyone. He hasn't watched a game since being sacked by his last club, West Bromwich Albion in September 1987. Instead, he now prefers to share his life with the Lord. He's turned his back on the game. Traded it in for religion.

For Kennedy, it's "game on". Whenever the subject turns to the Villa, his face lights up and having three West Midlands clubs in the top flight has only fired his enthusiasm. "It seems that Midlands football as a whole has been ignored by the sporting media in England. They try and bury us all the time, so it helps that we're all in the Premiership because we're always going to be in the spotlight," he said. "And by the way," he added hastily trying to make a point "there was nothing wrong with those Birmingham City fans running onto the pitch during the derby match. What was wrong was the fact that Villa got outplayed and lost. The atmosphere was amazing - it was a real game of football. Proper. Even though I was planning a different result, it was electric, man."

Musically he's surpassed every aspiration, but Kennedy does have one unfulfilled football fantasy.

"My dream is to watch my son play for Aston Villa," he said. "That would be phenomenal." He pauses for a moment. "Yeh man," he thinks again. "It would be much better than seeing him play the guitar to a full house at Symphony Hall - wouldn't it?"

Eyes down, and look in...

Saturday, November 16, 2002.

THE OLD LADY in the blue raincoat is flustered. Her "ring and ride" driver was late and if she doesn't get a move on she'll miss the first house. She scrambles around in her handbag. "It's no good," she tells Tracey on reception. "I've left my dabber at home. You'll have to lend me a felt tip."

It's 6.25pm on the Springvale Estate in Bilston. This is bingo land and business is steady for a damp Monday night. Another woman, who looks like Olive from *On the Buses*, places her order. "Ere yar, love," she says in a thick Black Country accent. "Early bird, main session, late session, flyer and six for the national." Among the regulars, a distinguished grey-haired gentleman stands partly hidden by a row of one-armed bandits. It's Dennis Mortimer - Aston Villa's 1982 European Cup-winning captain.

Mortimer proudly flashes his membership card. He's not a regular player, but he's gradually catching the bingo bug - as manager of Wolverhampton Wanderers women's team, he has no choice. "Two of the players' mums badgered me into it after one of our meetings at the Horse and Jockey pub," he said settling down for the first game of the night. One of those mothers, Denise Westwood, mother of Emily, the England international midfielder, is a bingo addict. "And," she said leaning over the table enthusiastically, "I come from the Priory Estate in Dudley - where Duncan Edwards was born."

A hush descends. It's eyes down, look in. We're playing for a line on the violet ticket and it's getting serious. Katrina, tonight's caller, begins. Five and two, 52. On its own, number two. "Come on Den, wake up. You've missed six and three 63," Denise said, frantically marking her own card while keeping a close eye on everybody else. "It's all right, my hand's just warming up," Mortimer replied.

The former Villa captain, who also played for Birmingham City and was assistant manager at West Bromwich Albion, is now a full-time coach-educator with the Professional Footballers' Association. He helps former professionals and young hopefuls become the big-name managers of tomorrow. But his role at Wolves Women, who are sponsored by Bilston toilet roll manufacturer J.Bishop, gives him as much satisfaction as anything he's done in the game. In women's football, even many of the leading names pay to play (subs are £4 a week) but the girls' enthusiasm is, in Mortimer's words, "quite unbelievable".

"The women's game is full of quality players and the expansion is phenomenal," he said. "I treat my team with respect. I'm not playing at it - I manage the girls in the same way as I would approach a job at the highest level, they wouldn't want to be treated different."

Mortimer hails from Kirkby in Merseyside, the son of Mary and Joseph. I'm about to ask him if he was born in a stable, but Katrina's off again. She's looking for a full house on the flyer. The prize is a family box of Quality Street.

"My Dad was a travelling salesman by day and managed a pop group by night, so we didn't see much of him," he said. There's confusion in the hall. Someone has "called a bogey" (It's when a punter shouts "house" incorrectly). Mortimer shrugs off the excitement: "But at least Dad made sure he took me and my four brothers to Anfield to watch Liverpool," he said.

That's where the Dennis Mortimer story begins.

He joined Coventry City as a 15-year-old, but his glory days came with Villa - and that night in Rotterdam. "Lifting the

European Cup was one of the best feelings you can have in the world," he said. "Our bonus was just £1,000 per man - ridiculous when you think about today's game. But money couldn't buy the feeling I had when I got my hands on the trophy. What more could a football player wish for?"

Mortimer gushes with pride when he talks about his days on top of the football world, but the moment doesn't last. Olive from *On the Buses* squeals "house". It's unfortunate. Mortimer was close to victory himself. He was sweating on top of the shop, 90, and two little ducks, 22. The money would have come in handy to boost funds for Wolverhampton Wanderers Women.

The conversation turns back to Aston Villa. The former captain feels he's been shunned by club chairman Doug Ellis since he ended his playing days. He was "totally devastated" when he was turned down for a job in the Villa community department, despite the backing of the FA. The rejection hurt him deeply.

A community job finally came up at Albion, however, and he rose to become number two to Keith Burkinshaw. "It was the opportunity I'd been waiting for. We had some great players, yet after just 18 months, we lost our jobs," Mortimer, who found out he'd been sacked when he read the local newspaper, said. When he asked Tony Hale, the Baggies chairman, why he'd been dismissed, the reply was, "Number twos always get the sack - don't they?"

Today Albion meet Villa at the Hawthorns. As a player, it's the fixture Dennis Mortimer looked forward to above any other. "For me, it was the big derby. We all enjoyed playing against Albion. We knew Blues fans hated us, but we felt the Baggies fans disliked us even more. And Albion had the better players. As a team we had to be at our best to win. With Blues it wasn't like that."

Today's game, according to Mortimer, will be settled on sheer passion. But he's unlikely to be watching. Instead he has

Wolves Women to think about. He's got a young squad and it's going to take every ounce of his coaching prowess to steer them into the Premier League.

He's trying every trick in the book to do it, too. "I've devised a bonus system," he said. "There's £10 for the player of the match, and if we go up at the end of the season they'll get all their subs back." There's a collective groan as the last full house of the night is claimed. A stream of unlucky punters head for home. But Mortimer is still deep in thought. "The girl who is nominated player of the match the most times will get a special prize," he added. "Although I haven't decided what that will be yet."

He thinks again: "It'll probably be a night at the bingo!"

Friday, May 16, 2003.

Dennis Mortimer launches a stinging attack on Aston Villa chairman Doug Ellis following the resignation of club manager Graham Taylor. Mortimer said:"I'm lending my name to get him removed. He's so far past his sell-by date it's untrue. It won't be easy but it has to be done. Our campaign will be ruthless, remorseless and relentless. When we get rid of Doug, I will lead a second personal campaign to have every trace of his name extinguished from Villa Park. When he arrived, Villa were the biggest club in the country - now they are not even the biggest club in Birmingham. Doug must go - it's as simple as that."

* Doug Ellis is still in control of Aston Villa. The Doug Ellis Stand, named by the chairman in honour of himself, remains at the ground.*

Why Lazaridis switched from swing to wing

Saturday, November 23, 2002.

IT'S CRUNCH TIME in cricket-mad Western Australia. The year is 1987 and a nervy teenager is about to be given the chance of a lifetime. The offer is tempting - yet he turns it down flat.

Cricket came easy to Stan Lazaridis, he was a natural. But his real passion has always been football. So for Western Australia, read Birmingham City. For the WACA, read St Andrew's. For the Ashes, read the Premiership.

Lazaridis still remembers the day when, at 16, he nailed his sporting colours to the mast once and for all. "I was asked to join a select side for the best young cricketers in Western Australia," he said. "That was the moment I had to make a choice - soccer or cricket. I told them I liked cricket, but I loved soccer and that was that, I left my cricket career behind that day. The same thing happened to Steve and Mark Waugh but they chose cricket over football."

Lazaridis was a left-arm fast bowler. He was spotted by former Australian Test player Bruce Reid who was helping to assemble the elite young team. "As a left arm pace bowler himself, he would have been the best man in the world to learn from," the Birmingham City winger said. "I'll never know how far I'd have gone in cricket. But I know I made the right decision and football is still my life. I never switch off from it," he added.

It's a cold, mucky Tuesday afternoon at Birmingham's Wasthills training-ground. It's almost 3pm yet the first-team squad are still being put through their paces. Life in the Premiership is not all fast cars and false-tanned beauties. The Abba hit *Fernando* blares out from the gymnasium. Steve Bruce, the Birmingham manager, barks out his orders. In the canteen they're serving the last few portions of chicken, bacon and cheese risotto. A sign on the notice board informs players that Monday is "weigh in day". There's a £50 fine for every kilo they are overweight. Outside, it's started to drizzle. No wonder Stan Lazaridis smiles when he talks of home.

"It gets hard, especially around Christmas, not having any family over here," he said, looking out of the canteen window. "I certainly miss the warm weather, the beaches, the sea and the sun - all things I took for granted. But it's a small sacrifice."

He's certainly come a long way. Lazaridis was the son of a Greek railway worker who migrated to Australia in the 1970s in search of a better life. The youngest of two boys, born and raised in Perth, he would make frequent trips with his family to the WACA ground to watch the Australian cricket heroes of the day. But while he worshiped the likes of Dennis Lillee and Rodney Marsh, he always dreamed of becoming a footballer like his hero John Barnes, the Watford and Liverpool winger. "In a way, I felt like I was the odd one out," he said.

His football fairytale began when he was just 6. "I went to watch my older brother, who was 10, play for Kingsway Olympic," Lazaridis said. "The team was short of one player and they asked me to make up the numbers." His whirlwind romance with the "funny English game" had started. "I played at state level when I was just 13 and made the Australia international team when I was 17. Everything happened so quickly."

When he was 20 Lazaridis, now a confirmed "Socceroo", moved to Adelaide to play at the highest level the country had to offer. He was paid just £100 a week and lived on meals of plain rice in a cold and uninviting basement flat without any furniture. He didn't mind. Chasing his football dream was all that mattered. Of course, he wasn't to know that the riches of the English Premiership were just around the corner.

"It was all a bit of a fluke," he said. "I was asked to play in an Aussie XI against West Ham United, who were on an end-of-season tour. I said I would turn out for nothing if they could get my family in to see the game free of charge. After the match Frank Lampard and Harry Redknapp asked me to go back to England. I'd never been to London before so I said I would give it a go." It was as simple as that.

"I landed on Sunday afternoon and by the Monday night I was playing against Chelsea's Ruud Gullit. I never planned it and I never thought for a moment it would happen," he said. "One moment I was a kid watching the games on television in Australia - the next I was playing myself. I was 23 but I was a young 23. Australian kids don't mature as quickly as the English. Life is a lot harder here and I found it incredibly difficult to settle in. But Harry Redknapp was always patient. He put his arm around me when he needed to, and hopefully, I repaid him in the years that followed."

Now Lazaridis is looking forward to going back to West Ham in February, when Australia play England in football's equivalent of the Ashes. It's going to be a special occasion for him and "absolutely massive for the folks back home", who regularly stay awake all night to watch "the boy" play. They're his number one fans.

Representing his country is a proud honour for Lazaridis. For a moment, his mind takes him back home again. These days, when he returns for real, he's treated like a hero. "I meet players of 16 who see me as a role model and that's fantastic," he said. "Do you know, I only have to look at a teenager's face to know if he's going to succeed or not. It's all in the look. I was there once. I had the look." He peers outside. It's still drizzling. "I like to spend time with those kids," he said. "I tell them. If I can do it - then so can you."

BRUM'S THE WORD

Wednesday, February 12, 2003.

The "folks back home" are sent into ecstasy when Stan Lazaridis sets up Australia's first goal in their stunning 3-1 win over England at Upton Park. Lazaridis' free kick saw Tony Popovic lose his marker to head past David James at the far post. Harry Kewell and Brett Emerton also scored for the Aussies while debutant Francis Jeffers pulled a goal back for the home side. Wayne Rooney became England's youngest international, making his debut at the age of 17 years and 111 days.

"Kanga-Poo! Stinking England dumped on by Aussies", screamed one national newspaper headline. Another read: "What a load of Roo-bish". A third reasoned: "Aussie's Rule. First cricket, then tennis, now this…"

West Bromwich Albion fan Brett Bensley, who ran onto the pitch wearing just a smile and a Union Jack posing pouch during the game, was later banned from all football matches for three years. Bensley, from Apollo Road, Oldbury, was also fined £100 with £69 costs by Stratford magistrates in east London after he admitted unlawfully encroaching on the playing area.

The hit man - and him

Saturday, November 30, 2002.

HIT MASTER PETE WATERMAN is ready for a battle. You can see it in his eyes.

The man who "invented pop" is sitting in the front room of a semi-detached house in Worcestershire, waiting patiently for a bacon and mushroom sandwich. It's his pre-match ritual whenever he visits the Midlands to watch his beloved Walsall. Today he's busier than usual. In a few hours he will be opening the new Purple Stand at the Bescot Stadium. Later he'll be watched by millions as the line-up of his new vocal harmony band One True Voice is revealed on ITV's *Pop Stars: The Rivals.*

But for the next few moments, his thoughts are dominated by one man: Ron Atkinson.

Waterman is hot favourite to claim a record fifth Christmas number one this year with his new band, but Atkinson, the former football manager turned crooner, has emerged as his unlikely pop rival. Now, for the first time, the Hit Man is going to hear what the Big Man has to offer.

Atkinson's single, *It's Christmas, Let's Give Love a Try*, will be released on December 9 and Waterman is keen to hear what he's up against. His ears are pricked. He's poised like a coiled cobra, both hands laid flat on a yellow tablecloth. He glares briefly at a simple crock butter dish in the centre of the dining table. For a moment, the room has become his makeshift Christmas number one battle headquarters. By way of a taunt, I cheekily dangle a "promotional copy" of Ron's Yuletide offering in front of Waterman's nose.

"Go on then, stick it on," he barks, getting anxious. Lips pursed, he studies the press release that accompanies Atkinson's first release. "It's a great feel-good song with a seasonal message in an era when the Christmas single has become nothing more than a cynical cash-in," it reads.

Atkinson doesn't burst into song. His offering has a more gentle beginning. He wrote the lyrics himself, although on the sleeve notes he gives credit to "his musical associate Cedric." Finally, Atkinson begins to sing:

> *Snowflakes falling all around.*
> *Sleeping children, make no sound.*

Waterman smiles. There's a hint of laughter. And then, slowly his head sinks into his hands. "Oh my God, it's dreadful," the man who made Kylie Minogue a pop megastar says.

Ron continues:

> *Rudolph's frosty breath leaves patterns in the sky.*
> *It's Christmas - Let's give love a try.*

Waterman is now open-mouthed. The bacon and mushroom sandwich arrives. He takes a bite, then, despairingly shakes his head. "The thing is," he says, as the room fills with the sound of hand bell ringing, "I don't know why anybody would do something like this. It must have cost him a bob or two," he smiles again. "I've never heard a record with so many out-of-tune vocals."

Tentatively, I ask the maestro: "Are you worried?"

"Not at all," he replies, ripping into another chunk of bread. "Big Ron's got as much chance of being Christmas number one as Walsall have of being top of the Premiership by the first of January. What label is it on - Tone Deaf Records?"

BRUM'S THE WORD

As a football fan, I'm not prepared to take any more. "But he's Ron Atkinson," I plead. "He's well loved."

Waterman's having none of it. "This song is like West Bromwich Albion - lacking in quality," he says, referring to one of Atkinson's former clubs. "I like the sentiment, but I've never heard so many clichés in one verse in my life." He takes another listen. "It might have been nice in 1952 with Max Bygraves singing it," he concedes.

Atkinson's love of music is legendary. It says so in the press release. He once organised a karaoke night for his Aston Villa players to relax them before a sixth-round FA Cup tie with Liverpool. The highlight of the night was Atkinson singing his version of *New York, New York*, entitled: "Dwight York, Dwight York".

"The karaoke machine has a lot to answer for in my business," the Coventry-born star-maker retorts. "Anyone who thinks they sound half-decent is egged on to make a record." Waterman stops, almost in mid-sentence. He's heard something he likes. "Hold on," he says suspiciously. "That's an oboe. Great instrument. It's a nice musical touch, that. It doesn't help the song, but at least it makes it more palatable."

Both *Pop Idol* and *Pop Stars: The Rivals* have taken their toll on Waterman. He's starting to feel the strain. Bosses at ITV have labelled him television's "new acceptable grey" - a successor to Des Lynam, perhaps. "They say I appeal to parents while still being cool in the eyes of the youngsters," he explains. The point was proved last weekend when he turned on the Coventry Christmas lights in front of more than 20,000 people. Kids that night where clambering to thrust their cassettes into his hands while their mothers were more inclined to embrace him. Now he's been asked to make a new series based on the old *Juke Box Jury* format. But he's put it on the back burner.

"I'm falling apart. Look at me - I'm 55 and I'm coming out in blotches," he says pulling up the sleeve of his blue check shirt to reveal a bare, yet blotchy forearm. "I've been on television continuously for almost three years," he adds. "With *Pop Stars: The Rivals* I'm not only a judge, I've written and produced the record and, if the boys have a problem at 3am in the morning, they call me. I've also got a Kylie album to consider - as well as my trainspotting and railway companies." (He's a railway fanatic).

"Besides," he adds breathlessly, "I need some football therapy."

That's where Walsall come in - and he's as passionate as ever.

"Football is a fantastic escape, even though we're getting hit by the injury-time sucker punch all too often this season," says Waterman, who watches The Saddlers with his friend and bodyguard, Joe Savage - the unofficial world bare-knuckle fighting champion, who comes from Bloxwich, in the heart of the Black Country.

For Atkinson, football is not just therapy. It's been a way of life since he signed for Aston Villa in May 1956 after being spotted as a useful inside forward for BSA Tools, a West Midlands amateur club. He never made the Villa first team and was given a free transfer in the late 1950s. As a manager, though, he soon found his feet. He had two spells at West Bromwich Albion, won the FA Cup twice with Manchester United and the League Cup with Villa, whom he also took to second place in the Premiership. On the Continent, he had just over 12 months managing Atletico Madrid.

On television, too, Big Ron the football co-commentator has sparkled. Like Waterman he's not afraid to have his say, although Atkinson's colourful grasp of the English language has lead to a whole new phenomenon: "Ronglish - The language of the gantry". He invented a new football phrase: "The Lollipop", used to describe a tricky winger weaving one or both feet over a stationary ball. His infamous football quotes include: "Well Clive, It's about the two Ms - movement and positioning." There's the classic: "He's not only a good player, but he's spiteful in the nicest sense of the word." And: "They've come out after half time and gone bang."

Now Waterman is tipping Atkinson's fledgling musical career to go bang. In the background, Big Ron has reached the last few lines of his song:

> *Love's the thing that money cannot buy.*
> *It's Christmas. Let's give love a try.*

The Hit Man has heard enough. I ask him what he would have made of Atkinson if they'd have come face to face in an audition for *Pop Idol*. "Just two words," he says. "No thanks!"

* *Pete Waterman's boy band One True Voice were beaten to the Christmas number one slot by their "pop rivals" Girls Aloud. The all-female group's offering, "Sound of the Underground" became the 50th Christmas chart topper since the hit parade began. It sold 213,000 copies compared to the boy's single, "Sacred Trust" that reached number two having sold 147,000.*

* *The Cheeky Girls - Transylvanian twins Monica and Gabriela Irimia - made it to number three with "Cheeky Song (Touch My Bum)".*

Remember.
You're a Womble

Wednesday, December 4, 2002.

PEOPLE DON'T NOTICE US, they never see. Under their noses, a Womble may be.

The Wayward Wombles, a barmy band of AFC Wimbledon supporters based in the West Midlands, are preparing to set off on a 300 mile round journey to watch their newly-formed team take on Chessington United in the Seagrave Haulage Combined Counties Football League.

The hardy group of 20 exiled, former Wimbledon FC supporters have raised £2,000 to sponsor the match.

Wayward Womble Martin Caswell, a Plough Lane regular since he was seven who now lives in Stafford, said: "We have withdrawn our support of Wimbledon in protest at the club's move to Milton Keynes. But we are fully behind the new AFC Wimbledon, and we are certainly not alone. Even though we've had to start all over again, the new club draws fans from all over the world. We average home gates of 4,000 while other teams in the same league attract only 15 or 20 fans - it's a magnificent football fairytale."

Caswell moved to the Midlands to take a job with the Health Protection Authority, but he is an avid AFC Wimbledon follower, along with his partner Rachel Halliwell. Their allegiance means they spend many long weekends "Wombling" to and from a cluster of humble football grounds in the Surrey area. "I sometimes wonder if we are dedicated fans or simply football nuts. How many supporters would travel so far to see a non-league game?" Rachel said.

AFC Wimbledon play at Kingsmeadow, in Kingston-Upon-Thames, a ground they are hoping to purchase in a bid to kick-start their assault on football glory. They need £2.5 million, but the supporters are determined to achieve their goal.

"I once went to Wembley Stadium to watch the old Wimbledon win the FA Cup Final against Liverpool," Caswell said. "Winning that game was a dream come true. I'm not dreaming now - I am certain that the new AFC Wimbledon will get into the Football League. I'm confident we will be in the Conference within five years. What's happening at Kingsmeadow is fantastic.

"In the Midlands alone, we've got Wayward Wombles in Wombourne, Wolverhampton, Cannock and Leamington Spa. Yes, we are the barmiest fans in the Midlands - but we don't mind the travelling. This is a real football story. Everyone who loves the game will surely appreciate what we are doing."

World tour: Nou Camp ...The Hawthorns

Saturday, December 7, 2002.

WHAT YOU LOSE on the roundabouts you gain on the swings. Take this week, for instance. First I'm called to book by Ron Atkinson, the budding pop star. Then, just two days later, I pull off a sensational deal with Russell "The Voice" Watson, the world-renowned tenor. Football. It's a funny old game.

Atkinson came to see me after reading Pete Waterman's scathing account of his debut single, *It's Christmas, Let's give Love a Try*. Waterman, who is also vying for the coveted Christmas number one slot with his boy band, One True Voice labelled Big Ron's offering as "dreadful" in this column last week. "I've never heard so many out-of-tune vocals in all my life," he said.

But Atkinson, who is relishing the prospect of a Yuletide showdown, was quick to hit back. "Pete has slipped up and he knows it," he said with a twinkle in his eye. "Being an avid Walsall fan, he should have realised that his team's greatest moments have come when they were underdogs - beating the big guns and upsetting the odds. I don't know what will come of my record but I know where I want it to be - and I love a contest."

Waterman predicted that his beloved Saddlers have more chance of being top of the Premiership by the beginning of January than Ron has of being Christmas number one - a point I mischievously put to Atkinson. He smiled his broad, Big Ron smile. When Atkinson grins, the room holds its breath. "Well, they are playing quite decent football at the moment," he said.

"Seriously," he added. "I'm a very lucky man. I've always loved whatever I've done in football, but making this record was one of the most enjoyable things of all. We just tried to capture the meaning of Christmas.

"The young pop stars are great, honestly they are. The kid David Gray is a fantastic singer, Oasis are terrific and Will Young has one hell of a voice - but you don't get traditional songs at this time of year any more. That's what we've tried to do. It's just another great adventure in my life."

Now Atkinson, whose song is released on Monday, is looking forward to appearing on Top of the Pops. "Or in my case, top of the grand-pops," he laughed like a drain, and then continued: "Tell Pete Waterman I'm planning a summer dance hit - a Foxtrot and a Lady's Invitation."

Atkinson, who rates Frank Sinatra as his undisputed musical hero, co-wrote *It's Christmas, Let's give Love a Try*, with Birmingham musician Cedric Whitehouse. They were perfecting the song until the bitter end, changing the last verse in the car on the way to the recording studios. Atkinson also altered a script for the video. "They wanted me to sing in the snow, then get into a limousine and travel around London with three scantily-clad ladies. I told them I wasn't having it, so the girls dressed up in Santa football kits instead."

For Atkinson, music has always been a welcome respite from the stresses of football. Often, he's managed to combine the two. He reckons he was one of the first people in the country to get a karaoke machine, and he regularly held "free-and-easy" nights for his players during spells at West Bromwich Albion, twice, Manchester United, Aston Villa and even Atletico Madrid where he worked for Jesus Gil, the Spanish club's erratic chairman. "You see," I quickly observed, "you've worked for Jesus. Surely that gives you a claim to a Christmas hit."

Wherever the game has taken him, though, he's always considered the Midlands to be home, and he's revelling in the area's football resurgence. He's even tipping former club Albion to successfully fight off the threat of relegation. "The one thing that impresses me is the way they fight for each other," he said. "Also, the fans won't turn against them and that will be a big plus - the atmosphere at The Hawthorns might keep them up."

That brings me nicely to Russell Watson.

Like Atkinson, "The Voice" is eagerly awaiting the release of a new record on Monday. In Watson's case, the album *Reprise* is promising to take "a completely different angle to Pavarotti or Placido Domingo". (Maybe Ron should have done the same).

The "people's tenor" spent eight years appearing "after the bingo" on the club circuit but sprang to fame when Martin Edwards, the Manchester United chairman, spotted him in a talent contest and asked him to sing at Old Trafford. He went on to perform in front of 92,000 at Barcelona's Nou Camp Stadium before United's unforgettable European Cup victory over Bayern Munich. When he sings, United excel. He has that effect on people. The Salford born former bolt cutter (he earned £90 a week before the secretary of the Wigan Road Working Men's Club suggested he tried singing "that Nesty Doormat") has sold more than 2.5 million albums, toured the world and entertained the Queen, American President George W. Bush and Pope John Paul II.

Now, I've persuaded him to sing for Albion in a desperate bid to keep them out of the Premiership's relegation zone. Our conversation went something like this:

Me: "Russell, can I book you?"

Watson (Somewhat surprised): "I beg your pardon Malcolm!"

Me: "Can I book you? You know. Singing! Would you consider coming with me to The Hawthorns and knocking out a couple of verses of *The Lord's My Shepherd*?"

Watson: "The Hawthorns? That's West Bromwich Albion's ground isn't it?"

Me: "Yes. They need something special to keep them out of the bottom three and *Psalm 23* is a sort of theme tune for the fans. What do you think? Can I book you one Saturday afternoon if you're not doing anything?"

Watson: "Go on then. Yes. Absolutely Malcolm. I'll be there for you, mate."

Me: "Do you know the words?"

Watson: "Yes, of course I do. *The Lord's my Sheperd, I shall not want. He makes me down to lie.*"

Me: "That's the one. I'll get a date and we'll fix it up."

Watson: "Thank you, Malcolm. Consider it done."

I could always ask Ron Atkinson as well. Watson has already successfully sung with Pavarotti, Sir Cliff Richard, Lulu and Lionel Richie. Who could resist the delicious combination of The Voice and The Mouth?

Are you watching, Waterman?

* *Donal Murray, via email, writes: "Lovely article on Big Ron. It brought a smile to my face this morning. I am a 33-year-old Baggies fan, currently living in Sydney, Australia. I originally hail from Belfast, Northern Ireland and have followed Albion for most of my life, much to the peculiar amusement of my friends.*

* *Ron Atkinson's single, It's Christmas, Let's Give Love a Try, failed to reach the Yuletide top twenty. Big Ron complained that he was robbed of a major chart hit because of distribution problems with the record. He's vowed to "try again" this Christmas.*

BRUM'S THE WORD

* Russell Watson maintains that he will keep his promise to sing at The Hawthorns, although his schedule prevented him from helping Albion avoid relegation.

Weir's heroes and Villans in compelling story

Saturday, December 14, 2002.

IT'S THE EARLY 1970s. A young boy queues patiently for his match-day programme. Dressed in a duffle coat, with an Aston Villa scarf wrapped tightly around his neck and a can of pop in his pocket for half-time, the lad eagerly holds out a ten pence piece. The look on his face is one of excitement and anticipation.

The boy's name is not known. He may not even support the club any more. It doesn't matter. In a split second, the photographer has captured the needs, hopes and dreams of a football generation. It's written all over the youngster's face. For the game's romantics this is more than a photograph. It's art in its highest form.

The image is one of more than 100 in a book by Terry Weir, who was Villa's official photographer for a quarter of a century. He saw the game through a lens during the Seventies, Eighties and into the Nineties. Almost every Weir picture tells a human story as well as a football one - often candid, sometimes comical, always compelling.

Turn a page of the book, entitled *The Weir and the Wonderful*, and you see a crowd of men in raincoats watching a game intently from the top of a rubble bank. This was Villa's old open terrace before the advent of seats, executive boxes and cantilever roofs. The shot throws up memories of a bygone age. It's all gone now, but Weir's work serves as a glorious reminder.

BRUM'S THE WORD

Another picture tells another story. This time, a scrawny teenage lad sells cheese biscuits from a refreshment tray that hangs awkwardly from his neck and rests heavily on his midriff. In the background the quaint half-time scoreboard nestles against an imposing floodlight pylon that dominates the corner of the ground. Turn again and a small girl in a tartan frock waves her flag in front of a packed terrace. The innocence of what was once "the people's game" is lovingly embraced on film by Weir and it's also etched on the faces of the Villa players of the day. Chico Hamilton, the club's midfielder, stands proudly outside his boutique in Wylde Green; naked goalkeeper Jim Cumbes receives a glass of champagne in the shower from manager Ron Saunders. Even "Pop" Ward, Villa's flat-capped tea man, is filmed for posterity.

Weir, from Great Barr, has always been a Villa fan. "I was born with claret and blue eyeballs," he said. His face is well worn. His life story told on a pinstripe waistcoat that bears an enamel Villa badge on one side and a small silver Laurel and Hardy statuette on the other. "Aston Villa, Laurel and Hardy and jazz. They're my three great passions," he confessed. "I named my daughter Louise after the great Louis Armstrong and I'm membership secretary of *The Gravy Tent*." (It's Birmingham's Laurel and Hardy Appreciation Society).

But football is where Weir has made his mark. He was a "two bit wedding photographer" when a mate offered him £14 plus expenses to cover his first match - Birmingham City verses Luton Town. "At first I turned him down flat being a Villa season ticket holder, but when he told me the fee I said: 'lead me to it.'"

By the start of the 1971-72 season, Weir had landed his dream job at Villa, who were then in the third division. "The commercial manager of the day, Eric Woodward, said he wanted me to photograph football. But on no account did he want to see a football in the pictures."

It was a weird yet wonderful request. And it worked like a dream. Soon Weir would become part of the fixtures and fittings at Villa Park. So much so that his personal copy of the book has been signed by Doug Ellis, the chairman. The inscription reads: "Thank you for your friendship over the last 30 years. Up the Villa!"

"Look at that," Weir said, suddenly thrusting page 95 in front of my nose. His finger is pointing to a laughing policeman who stands outside Villa's old Trinity Road Stand. The Bobby is getting on in years. He belongs to the good old days when an officer could afford a smile while still keeping law and order. "It was his last day of service," Weir explained. "I've just been contacted by his widow who has ordered four copies of the book for her grandchildren. It's a lovely way for them to remember their grandad.

"I often wonder where the people in my pictures are today. I'd love to meet some of them. In a way that would complete my days."

Weir combined his job as Villa photographer with his full time occupation as a technician at Aston University. The photography, though, became his passion - and it took him around the world covering Villa in what many consider the club's golden era. "My first trip abroad was to watch Villa in Antwerp," he said. "I'd only been as far as Dudley before. I didn't even have a passport."

Weir has flicked back to page 26. He stops to draw breath. It's a picture of Villa legend Tom "Pongo" Waring when he was an older gentleman. Waring's eyes are wide open, almost glaring. They tend to follow you around the room. "I took that picture at Tranmere Rovers one Friday night. It's very special. My dad used to worship him and he became my idol." For a moment, Weir is alone with his memories. "I was there when his widow scattered his ashes on the Villa Park pitch," he said. "It was the only time I ever put my camera away."

BRUM'S THE WORD

Now his camera has been put away for good. It hangs in the hall next to the hat he wore the night Villa won the European Cup in Rotterdam. In the garden he has three bricks from the old Holte End and the numbers four and six from the half-time scoreboard, although they now read 46 - the number of his house. Terry Weir doesn't need mementoes of his time at Villa, the memories are still fresh in his mind.

If he ever starts to forget, he need only glance through the pages of his "Weir and Wonderful" book.

* Dear Malcolm,

I have seen my name in print many times, but to be featured in your column in The Times was one of the nicest things that has ever happened to me. My minor celebrity status at Villa Park has never impressed my children, but, on hearing of your article, they drove around the shops to buy as many copies as they could. My daughter pinned the column on the wall at the shop where she works. She told every customer: "That's my dad". Unheard of reactions. Thank you for the boost you have given me.

Fraternally yours, Terry Weir.

Cisse prepares for a contrasting Christmas

Saturday, December 21, 2002.

"I'LL MEET YOU on the farm shop car park," a foreign sounding gentleman on the other end of the telephone says. "You'll know me. I'll be wearing a grey duffle coat down to my ankles and a blue check cap."

It is not a secret rendezvous. The man concerned is Roy Jones, chief sandwich maker for the Birmingham charity, Open Christmas, which feeds, clothes and temporarily houses 80 destitute people over the Yuletide period. He's also English teacher and translator to Aliou Cisse, the Birmingham City midfield player.

Jones is vital for the mission ahead. Cisse, Senegal's World Cup captain, hardly speaks a word of English, yet he has been embraced by the second city since his arrival from French club Montpellier at the start of the season - and it's not hard to see why. At the entrance of his Birmingham home, which is flanked by two huge concrete lions, (the lions of Senegal - not Aston Villa) Cisse stands with open arms and a charming smile. When you step into his house you become one of his friends.

But behind the smile there is a tragic story to be told.

Eleven members of Cisse's family, including his sister, perished in the *La Joola* ferry disaster off the coast of The Gambia in September. The way he conducted himself during his darkest days was admired throughout football. He even played in Birmingham's match against West Ham United before flying home to grieve - Steve Bruce, the Blues manager,

109

was under strict orders not to mention the tragedy to the rest of the squad until after the game. It was Cisse's way of dealing with the pain.

With Christmas just around the corner, Cisse is beginning to feel the hurt again. "I'm a family man," he said, speaking always through his interpreter. For a second or two, he stares at a basket of yellow roses on the fireplace. The smile has momentarily disappeared. "Family and football keep me going. Football is one half of me and family the other. Losing one relative is bad enough, but this? Nobody could possibly have been inside me and felt my tremendous grief. It's been so hard to take."

Having spent the whole of his career in the French leagues - he was spotted by Lille at the age of 13 and also appeared for Sedan and Paris Saint-Germain - Cisse has never played football over the Christmas period before. "Never, never, never!" he said. In France he would be enjoying a midwinter break and a traditional family gathering in Paris. "Christmas has always been a great time for us to come together," he explained.

That gathering will take place as usual this year, but it will be a sombre affair.

"At least it will give us time to reflect and pray for our family and the others who lost their lives in the disaster," Cisse said. "I won't be there, but I'll have the telephone. Then I'll go to bed and think about the Boxing Day game. It's going to be very, very strange. This year I can't spend Christmas the way I would like to.

"I'm a devoted believer and my faith has helped me enormously," he added. "But I'm glad I've got the game to fall back on. It gives me an opportunity to think of something else."

Football has been the salvation of Aliou Cisse many times over. As a boy, growing up in Zinguinchor, south Senegal, he never dreamt that he would play the game professionally, let alone lead his country to the quarter-finals of the World Cup.

"We lived on the streets," he said. "I kicked my first ball on the streets, grew up on the streets and learnt about life on the streets - the good, the bad and the ugly. For that reason, I'm very conscious of the great fortune I've had and the opportunity the game has given me. Football was my passion but I never played with an eye to becoming a professional. I played because I loved the sport."

At the age of 2, his parents emigrated to Paris leaving their young boy in the capable hands of his grandmother, Fatou. "But she didn't encourage my football at all," he said. "She wanted me to study, study, study and become an engineer or a lawyer. I had to play the game in secret."

With sheer determination, Cisse persevered. So began his emergence from street urchin to world-class sportsman. "On the quiet, while grandmother had her back turned," he worshipped English players such as Glenn Hoddle, Gary Lineker and, later, Steve Bruce - the captain of Manchester United.

Cisse, who is already proving to be an inspiration in the Premiership for Birmingham, still thinks highly of the man he once admired from afar. "He's a special manager. One who cares for his players. And he's got the club working in a professional way," he said. "With five months gone we are doing well, but the hardest part of the season is still to come and that's why the transfer window is so vital. We need to make some additions to the squad - *special players*."

Bruce is not the only reason why Cisse feels at home in the West Midlands. He has developed a love affair with the Birmingham City fans who turned the whole of the Tilton Road End of St Andrew's into a huge Senegal flag as a special "welcome home" when he returned after taking time off in the aftermath of the tragedy. Sparkbrook printers HW Owen provided the coloured cards free of charge.

Cisse will never forget that day. "It was so important that I didn't feel alone at that time," he said. "Fortunately I had lots of people to support me, the team management, the players and above all the fans. They were incredible. That's why I will always give everything for this team. Heart and soul. At any club, the fans are the real connoisseurs of the game - at Birmingham they are there for us, no matter how we perform. As players it's up to us to take on that responsibility and reward them."

As I leave Cisse, I wish him a merry Christmas. "*Bon Noel*," he replied with that smile. I hope he has a happier new year.

* Karl Collier, via email, writes: "Thank you for writing about Aliou Cisse in The Times. I read the article over and over. He is a credit to my club and the way he has dealt with his family tragedies is nothing short of super-human. Thank you again for writing such a moving, informative and heart-warming column. Merry Christmas."

* John Baker, via email from Boise, Idaho, writes: "Brilliant piece of work, Malcolm. Many thanks for that."

* During the transfer window, Steve Bruce added French World Cup forward Christophe Dugarry to his Birmingham City squad - a "special player".

Christmas morning

Wednesday, December 25, 2002.

AN ASTON VILLA mirror hangs above the office desk. Glance out of the window, and you can see the towering stands of Newcastle United's St James' Park. It's Christmas Day in the northeast, football's fatherland.

Methodist minister, the Reverend Leo Osborn, stops for a second to catch a fleeting glimpse of himself in that Villa mirror which has pride of place in his study, he can afford a smile. Life is good. An unmistakable Yuletide feeling of peace and goodwill fills the air - and he's just received the greatest Christmas present of all time.

As chairman of the Newcastle district of Methodist churches, Rev. Osborn looks after 195 places of worship in the north of England. He's the Methodist version of a Bishop, and the run-up to Christmas has been an exceptionally busy time. As an Aston Villa fan, he's a long way from home, but he still adores his boyhood team. As a football supporter he stands alone, he's a one-off. The unique Christmas gift, which he bought for himself, is a leather-bound bundle of Aston Villa programmes. To Rev. Osborn, they are priceless. They complete his stunning collection. He now has every Villa match-day magazine that was ever printed - from 1906 to date.

"Volume one, issue one. September 1, 1906," he says, caressing his prized possession. "It cost one penny in those days, but please don't ask what I've just paid." He flicks through the delicate pages. A glossy picture of "gentle" Howard Spencer, the prince of fullbacks, graces the front. Inside, there are adverts for Vaughton's Medals and Badges in

Livery Street and Henry Riley's Piano and Organ Emporium in Constitution Hill.

"The reading material is amazing," he said. "Twelve pages of solid print and the early programmes also commented on world events. It's a catalogue of social history. There's even a regular piece on the Aston Villa Cricket team of the day. I love going through them. It's a wonderful feeling knowing my collection is finally complete. It's taken a long time, but it's a magnificent Christmas present."

Rev Osborn's Villa story began as a boy of 7. The family lived on Church Road in Handsworth, exactly half-way between Villa Park and The Hawthorns. "I asked my dad who we were going to support and he replied 'Villa, of course', so we went down the road rather than up the road for our first game."

He still remembers that match vividly. "It was Holy Saturday 1960, against Bristol City," he said. "We won 2-1 thanks to a pair of Stan Lynn penalties and the victory secured the club's promotion back into the first division. I remember, I swung my rattle around with such gusto that it knocked off a gentleman's hat in front of us."

His fascination for football programmes began around the same time. His most treasured match-day magazine cost him just ten pence. "It's got nothing to do with Aston Villa, though," he said. "The game is Sheffield Wednesday against Manchester United - the first match after the Munich Air Disaster. The Sheffield team is printed in full, but there are no names down for the United side.

"Apart from that, I treasure my European Cup Final programmes when Villa beat Bayern Munich in 1982. They printed two on the night for some reason and I've got them both. I'm proud to say that I was in Rotterdam and it was a wonderful occasion, I'll never forget it," he stops to sort through another pile. He has more than 5,000 match-day magazines of all shapes and sizes covering nearly 100 years of football action. Each one tells a unique story of how fashions have changed over the decades - along with the game itself. They take up acres of space in a four-bedroom manse that he shares with his "understanding" wife, Charlotte. "I used to have every FA Cup Final programme from 1923 to the present day," he said. "But I had to get rid of those to raise funds to complete my Villa collection."

He picks out another special memento - it's the programme for Villa's away game at Arsenal on May 2, 1981, when the team secured the league championship.

"This brings back such lovely memories," Rev. Osborn, who is a member of the "92 club", and has watched Villa on 64 grounds around the world, said. "We had an important Methodist synod that day - it was a six-line whip. Everybody had to attend. But I grovelled to the Minister. He told me, 'I can't possibly give you permission to attend a football match.' Then, he thought for a second and added 'I suppose your club hasn't won the league for 71 years - and it'll be another 71 years before they win it again. So you'd better be off.'"

Rev. Osborn's undying love for Villa has continued even though he left the Midlands to become a male nurse in Norwich at the start of the 1970s. He knew from the age of 4 that he would one day enter the clergy; "I didn't want to be a spaceman or a train driver, I wanted to commit my life to Christ," he said.

But joining the nursing profession en-route, was the best thing he ever did. "It taught me how people lived their lives. I had to deal with death, illness and ordinary folk asking me almost every day, 'how on earth can there be a God?' It was excellent training."

Finally he settled in Newcastle. His home nestles in the shadows of St James' Park. His Methodist patch extends from Berwick in the north to Sunderland in the south. His adopted parishioners have grown to love him. The feeling is mutual. Everyday he mingles with "fanatical football folk".

"They take the game very much to heart," said Rev. Osborn, who is also chaplain for the Albany Northern League, the second oldest football league in the country. "Even if I knew nothing about football, I would still be able to tell whether Newcastle or Sunderland had lost on Saturday. You can feel it coming back at you in church the day after a game. A defeat for the team here is a defeat for the whole community. It's a matter of pride.

"Of course, they can't understand why I'm an Aston Villa fan," he added sheepishly. "At first I get a bewildered stare - and then they tend to take pity on me."

Albert Tripp's pigs

Saturday, December 28, 2002.

THERE WAS A FARMER who lived in Dudley. At 12.30pm every day he would get a large stick and chase his pigs around their pen until he could barely stand through exhaustion. At 1.15pm he would carve off a piece of crusty bread and wipe it on the backs of his sweating animals - that was his lunch.

The farmer's name was Albert Tripp and he claims to have invented pork dripping. When his pigs perspired, it was time to eat.

Tripp wasn't a good-looking fellow. Some said he had a face like a dropped pile. His wife Molly had a terrible time with him. "She had to take him everywhere twice," they said. "The second time to apologise." Still, Albert Tripp had the fittest pigs in the Black Country.

Tripp adored pigs. He loved West Bromwich Albion too. He used to stand underneath the old half-time scoreboard on the Woodman Corner, Albion's only section of open terrace. Tripp was in his element when exposed to the harsh weather. There was nothing he liked better than watching his beloved Baggies slump to another mid-winter defeat while being pounded by a relentless band of driving sleet. It made him feel good. He was also well known at The Hawthorns for his unique battle cry. When an Albion player had the ball, you could hear him, sometimes above a 50,000-plus crowd, yelling: "GET RID OF IT!" Wherever the player was on the field, whatever his chances of scoring, Tripp's advice was always the same.

He was a generous man, though, and that made him very popular at this time of year. It was a tradition in the Black Country to have a pig at the start of January and keep it in a makeshift pen in the backyard. The animal would be slaughtered the following Christmas after eating a good year's supply of Grorty Dick (a sort of lentil porridge). The pig would keep the family fed for the next 12 months. Times were hard, and Tripp would often give away one of his animals to help a struggling family in the difficult months ahead.

He also made his own faggots - and this was where Tripp really came into his own. It was only a sideline, but legend has it that he once delivered two dozen to Vic Buckingham, the Albion manager, shortly before a Christmas Day fixture against Liverpool in 1953. He told Buckingham to make sure each player ate a faggot before the match. Albion won 5-2 (Nicholls, Griffin 2, Barlow and Allen).

Tripp is dead now, but he would have been a proud man this winter. The first sleet of the season is beginning to fall, his beloved Baggies are again spending Christmas in the company of football royalty, Arsenal - and, to cap it all, Fred and Janet Doody from Dudley, along with son Lewis and daughter Gemma, have been named Britain's Faggot Family 2003.

The Doodys, who are also staunch West Bromwich Albion supporters, will be the face of Mr Brain's Faggots for the next 12 months. Their family picture already graces the company's Christmas card.

Fred Doody's passion for Albion began 30 years ago. His most treasured possessions are an autographed Albion ball and a section of turf ripped from Oldham Athletic's Boundary Park pitch the day the Baggies won promotion in 1976. He keeps the grass in a shoebox in the front room. Fred started watching Albion's matches underneath the half-time scoreboard on the Woodman Corner.

His passion for faggots has also been a lifelong affair. The family became the new face of the faggot when Fred's mother, Gladys, spotted an advert in a local newspaper. They faced stiff competition from all over the country but came through after negotiating a series of, according to a company press release, "tests, faggot role-plays and quizzes". Christine Hamilton was one of the judges.

Now the family face a hectic spell travelling around the United Kingdom preparing "ordinary shoppers" for National Faggot Week at the end of January. On top of that, they're being constantly followed by a team of BBC documentary makers. The story of the faggot family is due to hit the screens in March. "It's a case of stand aside OXO family, the Doody's are on the march," Janet said in her broad Black Country accent.

You would be forgiven for thinking that this is a simple, heart-warming Yuletide tale and that all is well for Albert Tripp as he blissfully chases his pigs around a heavenly pen in the clouds. But there's a problem in faggot land. Fred feels partly responsible for Albion's miserable position in the Barclaycard Premiership this season, and it's all to do with the autographed football. "At the start of the season it started to go down," Janet said. "I told Fred to pump it up because I've got a feeling that if the ball goes down, then so will the team. He put some wind in it and Albion won three on the bounce."

Fred, a local market trader, begins to frown. "But we've been so busy promoting faggots that I haven't had time to keep pumping up the ball," he said. "It's starting to worry me. I feel the team's performance is all down to the ball. I might even have to take it around the country with me on our promotional tours. Either that or give the Albion team a year's supply of faggots."

If the ball stays inflated the family are convinced the team will stay up. If it starts to go down, the Baggies will slide. Life, for football fans, is sometimes as simple as that. Of course, Tripp's advice would be: "GET RID OF IT", but that's out of the question. The faggot family's ball could hold the key to Albion's season. After all, the Doody's are fed up watching their side running around week after week building up a sweat so that the Premiership's big boys can feed off their backs. That makes them no better than Albert Tripp's pigs.

* *Michael Bingham, via email from Lympsham, Somerset, writes: "Being Dudley born and bred, I can personally vouch for the veracity of the origins of Albert Tripp's 'pig-sweat' dripping. It was said that extra salt was needed to bring out the full flavour on a piece of warm, freshly baked bread. Tripp was also famous for dangling his younger pigs over the farm walls whenever the Dudley Salvation Army Band marched past so they could gain an appreciation for music."*

Mitchell's knee in the groin for all true Blues

Saturday, January 4, 2003.

THE WHISPER OF HIS NAME strikes fear into the soul of every Birmingham City fan. His presence alone made Jasper Carrott go to pieces on the golf course. He turned one family's Spanish holiday upside down when he began ball juggling on the beach. A taxi driver from Chelmsley Wood swears he will never accept his fare. When he sets foot in the West Midlands, he arrives incognito.

He is John Mitchell. And, although it may come as a dreadful shock to the blue-and-white half of the second city, he's a very nice man.

In 1975, Mitchell's knee cruelly knocked Birmingham City out of the FA Cup in the last seconds of their semi-final replay at Maine Road. He shattered the dreams of a football club who, in their centenary season, had already written the Wembley script. They've never forgotten it at St Andrew's. Most of them never will.

It was 9.47pm on April 9 when Mitchell struck. *Bye Bye Baby* by the Bay City Rollers was half way through a six week run at the top of the charts. In the cinemas, *Jaws* was about to become the box office hit of the year, while youngsters throughout the land were hooked on the ball-bearing shooting game called Crossfire.

At the risk of upsetting a generation of Blues supporters still dreaming of their first FA Cup final victory, here's how it happened - in the words of the man himself.

"It was the worst goal of my career," Mitchell, who now runs his own golf business near Luton, said. "But it was also the most important.

"It's so vivid in my mind. It was a typical grey Manchester evening, the pitch was muddy and, on the night in question, Blues were by far the better side. There was nine seconds of extra time left when Alan Slough picked up the ball on the right-hand side of the field. I knew it was going to be the last chance of the game. Being Sloughie, I also knew exactly what he was going to do - a little nudge to the right then a long, clipped diagonal ball towards the touchline. I took a gamble, span myself round and raced towards goal.

"Dave Latchford, the Blues goalkeeper, was coming towards me but I managed to get a decent toe-poke onto the ball with my right foot. The ball hit Latchford, came off my knee and gently rolled towards goal. I'm on the floor thinking, 'that's never going in'. But somehow the ball gathered a bit of pace and Joe Gallagher, the Birmingham defender who was chasing back, stumbled. He seemed to have lead in his boots. In the end I think I blew it in.

"When the ball finally crept over the line I knew we had won the game. One thought came immediately into my mind: Wembley! And for Fulham, that was Utopia."

Blues barely had time to restart the match. Any lingering hopes of a long awaited trip to the twin towers evaporated before their fans' now tearful eyes - and it was all Mitchell's fault.

"In that split second I achieved folklore status in both West London and the West Midlands. I had the most infamous knee in the game," he said. "For Fulham fans the goal was so special, but after the final whistle I saw the Birmingham winger Gordon Taylor, now chairman of the PFA, crying his heart out in the tunnel. It was his last chance of appearing in an FA Cup Final, and he knew it. Seeing him made me realise there were two sides to the story."

Eight years later, on a beach in Tenerife, Mitchell discovered how, like elephants, true football fans never forget.

"It's amazing how it keeps cropping up," he said. "I was playing football with a family on the sand and the dad asked me if I played the game professionally. You could tell by his accent he was a Brummie through and through. When I told him I was John Mitchell, his face dropped. He never spoke to me again. His wife told me that his holiday had been ruined when he discovered who I was."

The comedian Jasper Carrot, Birmingham's most famous fan, also suffers from the recurring "Mitchell nightmare" syndrome.

"I bumped into him on a golf course a couple of years ago. I introduced myself and he just starred blankly at my face before screaming 'B*****d!' His game went to pieces that day and, of course, he blamed me. I still have to wear dark glasses and a hat if I'm going to Birmingham but it's mostly good humoured," he said.

Mitchell was destined to play football, following in the footsteps of his father Alec, the England amateur international. His career began with non-league St Albans before a dream move to Fulham. On his 21st birthday he "nutmegged" Pele while playing for the Cottagers against a touring Santos side. The 1975 Cup team, who eventually lost 2-0 to West Ham United in the final, also included Alan Mullery and the late Bobby Moore who became Mitchell's great friend. "The nicest man I have ever met in my life," he said. "I still miss him terribly."

Moore and Mitchell shared a bottle of champagne in the bath the night Fulham knocked out Birmingham. Tomorrow afternoon, 28 years on, the two sides face each other again in the FA Cup at Loftus Road. It's their first Cup meeting since that fateful night at Maine Road. For some, time has stood still.

BRUM'S THE WORD

Paul Collins, a Birmingham taxi driver, will certainly have revenge on his mind. He was a ten year-old Blues fanatic when "that forward in a red-and-black striped shirt" made him cry. A poem, *John Mitchell is His Name*, still hangs in his black cab. Mitchell is the only man he would refuse point blank to pick up.

The poem reads:

> *His goal broke my heart and the tears I cried.*
> *But my love for the Blues has never died.*

Collins has scrawled two more lines onto the bottom of his now grubby sheet of lined writing paper:

> *So now to the present to settle the score.*
> *Let's do it for Steve Bruce and go one round more.*

* John Mitchell and the 1975 Fulham squad became pop stars when they performed their FA Cup Final song on Top of the Pops before their big day out at Wembley Stadium. The ditty, "Viva el Fulham", was written to the tune of the 1974 summer hit"Y Viva Espana". It contained the lyrics:

> *Oh this year we're going to win the Cup.*
> *Hey viva, elFulham.*
> *Next year, you know we're going up.*
> *Hey viva, el Fulham.*
> *Alan M is a wonder that's for sure.*
> *Hey viva, el Fulham.*
> *And Bobby? Well, do we need say Moore.*
> *It's Fulham por favor.*

Want to know about Villa? Jack's the lad

Saturday, January 11, 2003.

A DISTINGUISHED ELDERLY GENTLEMAN waits patiently at a bus stop in Erdington. He glances at his watch. If he's lucky, the 107 will be on time and he will be at Villa Park within 30 minutes. If he is extra lucky, Doug Ellis, the Aston Villa chairman, will pass by in his Rolls-Royce and give him a lift. Welcome to the extraordinary world of 84-year-old "Sir" Jack Watts.

It is a bitterly cold morning but Jack doesn't dither as the north wind doth blow. He's wrapped up in his official Villa anorak. On his club blazer, there is a simple gold badge that reads, "Jack Watts. Tour Guide". That's his job three days a week, taking football fans around the ground that Doug built. A Villa fan for 80 years, Jack worships Doug. "He looks after me well," Jack says. "I have a turkey off him every Christmas without fail. And if he ever sees me at the bus stop, he'll pull over and take me to work." Underneath his Captain Mainwaring-style moustache, there is a hint of a grin. "He's the best chairman in the land - and he's got a lovely Rolls-Royce."

Jack Watts is a walking Villa encyclopaedia. As one of the club's most trusted and loyal servants, he has access to all areas of the ground. He leads me into executive box six in the North Stand. "It'll give us a few minutes peace and quiet," he says.

Of course, it needs more than a few minutes for his story to be told.

"First game, 1922." He starts off like a sergeant-major. "But the best match I ever saw was against Arsenal ten years later, when 17 internationals graced the pitch - the cream of world football." Jack was just 14, but he remembers the surname of every player on the field that day and rattles them off one by one. The Villa captain was England skipper Billy "Knocker" Walker. He's still Jack's idol.

"I've got a doll who sits in Villa colours on the settee at home. We call him Knocker," he says. "It's my tribute to Billy. He was the greatest."

The doll was knitted by Jack's wife, Edna. They've been married for 63 years, but then loyalty is Jack's middle name - 80 years supporting the same club, 63 years with one "good lady" and 48 years working as "superintendent of the stores" at Samuel Taylor, the Midlands manufacturing firm. "They've gone bump now," he said, raising his eyebrows to the clear blue sky. "Birmingham. It was the city of a thousand trades - now it's all gone thanks to these lot," Jack adds referring to the current Government. "I'd like to get Tony Blair down here and tell him what I think of him."

Jack's first job at Villa Park was cleaning the seats in the main stand. "I started the week before World War Two broke out," he recalls. "One minute we were playing Everton at home and the next the King sent for me. He said, 'Do you want to have a knock at the Germans, Jack?' 'All right, George,' I replied, and that was that."

After the war, Jack worked behind Villa's half-time scoreboard at the Holte End, a post he held for 35 years until it was demolished in 1981. He only ever missed one match, a "friendly" with Glasgow Rangers when police were forced to close the scoreboard down after a bottle was thrown at the operators by visiting fans.

"I loved that job," he says. "We had the best view in the ground - and I made it my mission to get the scores up before the Villa players left the field for their half-time cup of tea." He stops suddenly. A memory has stirred in his always-active football head. "I almost came a cropper once," he whispers in case anyone is listening. "I dropped one of the numbered metal plates on to a supporters head." Jack shudders for a moment. "I thought I'd get the sack, but luckily the fan turned out to be an old school friend and took no further action. He was wounded, but they made them tough in them days."

Now on match days, Jack looks after the chairman's "special guests" in the new Trinity Road Stand. When it was opened by the Prince of Wales in December 2001, Jack was one of the dignitaries. He fully deserved his place in the official party, having stood on Aston Park with his brother in 1924 watching the Duke of York open the old stand.

"Prince Charles stopped to talk to me," Jack says proudly. "He said, 'I believe you knew my grandfather?' I was as pleased as punch." Jack stops again to adjust his bi-focal glasses and stare briefly at his watch. Today's tour is about to start and there is a group ready and waiting in Villa's Corner Flag restaurant.

Now Jack the Villa fan becomes Jack the Lad. "Are you all from Birmingham?" he asks the morning's punters by way of a warm-up routine. They're not, one couple have travelled from Newcastle. "Geordies!" Jack responds, as quick as a flash. "I was there during the war in 1944 - finest people I ever met. Used to go dancing at the Oxford Galleries."

Jack starts the tour by looking at a beautiful model of Villa Park as it was in 1962. "We had our record attendance on this ground, 76,588," he says to his attentive audience. "The year was 1946 - we lost by four goals to three to Derby County." The master is in full flow, every fact at his fingertips.

"Unfortunately the old Trinity Road stand has now been demolished, much to my regret," he adds.

Jack Watts looks straight into my eyes. "I'm not sure if you should put that last bit in," he says nervously. "It was Doug who knocked the bloody thing down."

* *Steve King, via email from Bathampton, Somerset, writes: "What a lovely article - especially for a life long Villa fan. I was a 14-year-old standing in that crowd of 76,588 in 1946, together with my friend - it was a wonderful game. It was also, however, quite a frightening experience for boys of our size and weight.*

"Every time there was exciting goalmouth activity, the crowd surged forward and we were carried along with them, off our feet, with no control over our movements. With about 15 minutes to go, when Villa were leading 3-2, we decided to leave to get into the queue for the 3X tram back to the city centre. As we left the ground, we heard a great roar - and then another. We bought a pink Sports Argus in the city centre and found out that we had lost 4-3. "

* *Alan Connolly, via email, writes: "Just a short note to say how much I enjoy your Brum's the Word column in The Times. However, you can imagine my shock when I read that the company Samuel Taylor had 'gone bump'. I have been employed at Samuel Taylor as quality assurance manager for the last 12 years. We employ 65 people and are currently exporting 50 per cent of our production of precious metal contacts.*

"I turned up for work this morning full of trepidation - but all was well and we are still here.

"Like Jack Watts, I am a true Villain. I will be happy to show him around Samuel Taylor's new site in Redditch in exchange for a tour around Villa Park. "

In memory of The King

Saturday, January 18, 2003.

LARAINE ASTLE makes no attempt to fight back the tears.

Her world fell apart a year ago when her husband Jeff, West Bromwich Albion forward, England international and gentleman, died from an "industrial disease". Heading a leather football damaged his brain beyond repair. The game he loved had killed him. Albion fans lost their "king". Laraine lost everything.

She said goodbye to her "angel" on January 19, 2002. He was 59. The day afterwards, you could almost feel the grief as thousands of Albion fans turned up to watch their team play Walsall at The Hawthorns. The shocking news of Jeff Astle's death reduced many to tears. The match was overshadowed by an overwhelming sense of loss around the ground. A year on, Laraine Astle still feels the pain as keenly as ever. "I've been dreading this weekend more than anything in my whole life," she said reliving the memories of 12 months ago.

"I can see Jeff now sat quietly on the settee, his big blue eyes looking up at me," she added. "It's one of my last memories of him. It was Jeff Astle but not the great footballer people would instantly recognise - his face was grey, he was really poorly. I got down the picture of him scoring the FA Cup Final winning goal in 1968 and asked him if he remembered it. I often did that, trying to keep his brain active. Sometimes his face would light up. But on this day, I looked deep into those eyes and they were tired. 'Who did you play for?' I asked. He took a while to think and then finally replied: 'Was it Fulham?'

"'No my darling,' I said, taking hold of his hand. 'It was West Bromwich Albion.' I will never forget that moment. At times I can still hear his voice and those three words: 'Was it Fulham?' That's when I realised he was slipping away."

Astle signed for Albion from Notts County in 1964. He went on to become a Hawthorns legend, scoring 174 goals in 361 senior appearances for the club and representing his country five times. It's one of the game's sad ironies that he's often remembered for a chance he missed - for England against Brazil in the 1970 World Cup. Having run a successful window-cleaning business after his retirement from football, he came back into the public eye in the 1990s with his tongue-in-cheek singing slot with Frank Skinner on the *Fantasy Football League* television programme.

Today, his England caps hang in the living-room of the couple's home near Burton-upon-Trent, alongside the shirt he wore when Albion beat Everton 1-0 to win the FA Cup. Above the fireplace is the picture of his winning goal. He went into the record books that season for scoring in every round. Laraine has been helped through her darkest days by the support of Albion fans from around the world. "They've been a tower of strength," she said. She has even been created a vice-president of the supporters' club.

But what she calls a wall of silence from the game's authorities has left her angry and determined to fight for "justice and compensation". Last month, she instructed her lawyers to begin legal action against the FA. That could lead to a test case in the High Court. She is ready for a long legal battle - a fight that could ultimately open the floodgates for other former players who are suffering from degenerative illnesses such as dementia and Alzheimer's disease.

Laraine, always dignified in her grief, said: "I know it's not going to be pleasant but nothing could be worse than watching my husband slip away before my eyes.

"People haven't got a clue what we went through. It broke my heart, but I made it my mission to protect Jeff's dignity. I was determined he would never end up in a home and I didn't want people to see him deteriorate. Hardly a soul knew he was ill. I wanted them to remember Jeff as he was. That's why I looked after him for 24 hours a day, seven days a week. His was the loneliest disease in the world and I lived a nightmare. I'd have sold everything to make him better. I'd have lived in a tent to give him the best treatment but there was nothing I could do.

"When I was shown the post-mortem results I broke down in tears. I knew in my heart that football had killed Jeff, but this was the proof," she said. "The FA can't say that football didn't kill him, yet I've had no communication from them since the verdict. All I want is someone in the game to hold up their hands and say, 'yes - although we never wanted this to happen - your husband died from heading a leather football.' That would give us all great comfort. But they've tried to sweep it under the carpet."

Compensation is of secondary importance to Laraine. She would put most of any cash award away for her grandchildren "so they could have a present from their granddad in years to come". She is also keen to help the Dovedale Respite Centre where Jeff was looked after so wonderfully during his last months.

The real motivation behind her legal crusade is to fulfil a last promise she made to her husband. She explained: "On the Saturday he died I remember him trying to attract my attention. He wanted a kiss but he had forgotten the word for kiss so he mimed the action. It was heartbreaking. I went over and gave him a big cuddle.

"I kissed him again, for the last time, as he lay in the Chapel of Rest. I wrapped my arms around him and promised I would get him justice. It was the hardest thing I have ever had to do. But I'll get it, even if it takes every penny. He's too decent a person to be forgotten.

"I've got truth on my side and, in a way, I'm no different from a miner's wife or an asbestos worker's wife. Jeff died from an industrial disease and I owe it to his legacy to put the record straight for him and others who suffered. Only then can the healing process begin.

"They say time is a great healer - it's wrong. Although you learn to cope over a period of time, I don't think my pain will ever heal. He was my angel. My only small comfort is that he never forgot who I was. Also, he didn't realise he'd got the disease. He was always so full of fun, so laid back. The illness robbed him of that and turned him into everything he wasn't. He'd have hated it."

Laraine and Jeff would have celebrated their 40th wedding anniversary this year. She met him at a miners' welfare club in Nottingham when she was just 15. He was a 19-year-old Notts County apprentice, learning to head a ball alongside the great Tommy Lawton.

"All of my family supported Forest," Laraine who now wears her husband's wedding ring on her right hand, said. "He was so shy as a teenager. He'd spend all night over a pint of Mackeson. Finally he got his mate 'Jogger' Holmes to ask if he could walk me home. Our first date was at the cinema. We ate ham salad and watched *The Longest Day*."

They were married in December 1963. That has made the Christmas and new year period especially difficult for the Astle family." His absence stood out," Laraine said. "Half of me was missing. It was awful. I was in my house, but without Jeff it wasn't my home. In a way I wished someone could have given me an injection and put me to sleep over the festive period and woken me up after the anniversary of his death. This weekend is going to be my biggest hurdle.

"My mother Maggie died suddenly eight days before Jeff. I think she might have looked down on him and saw how poorly he was. I can almost hear her saying: 'Come on me duck, you've suffered enough. You're coming with me.' It was funny because all the family were there when he died which was very rare indeed. It was his daughter's birthday. I'm convinced my mum came for him."

Again Laraine's mind flashes back to South Staffordshire coroner Andrew Haigh's verdict of last November. Degenerative brain disease brought on by heading heavy footballs. "An industrial disease," she said repeating his dramatic conclusion. "The words still haunt me. I often remember how we all stood and cheered when he headed the ball. We didn't know it was killing him. People often say that he would have played the game even if he was aware of the dangers, but I know he wouldn't. We became friendly with the world middleweight boxing champion, Richie Woodhall, who is a big Albion fan. I remember Jeff telling me he wouldn't let any lad of his take up boxing because of the damage it can do to the brain. I hear those words time and time again in my head.

"It proves Jeff would never have headed the ball if he knew it would one day rob him of his life."

Laraine has not visited The Hawthorns since Jeff's death. She is saddened that the club he served so loyally has not been in contact since the coroner's verdict. Albion had originally promised a tribute to mark the first anniversary of Jeff's death. Laraine's heard nothing. It only adds to her hurt. She freely admits to not having slept properly since he was diagnosed four years ago. The stress and shock has left her with rheumatoid arthritis.

Laraine picks up a letter from an Albion fan who lives in Rowley Regis. The envelope is addressed:

BRUM'S THE WORD

Mr Postman. Please help me!
Laraine Astle,
Widow of Jeff Astle,
Somewhere near Burton,
Derbyshire.

"I just want you to know," Laraine said, reading the note. "Your husband is not forgotten and never will be. I always wanted to be 'The King', to score great goals and wave my arms to the crowd. Although I never knew him, he was my hero and my mate. I've told my four-year-old son about him. When he said his prayers last night he finished with: 'Oh, by the way - God bless Jeff Astle.'" A picture of Jeff, drawn by the boy, accompanies the letter.

"This gives me the strength to go on," Laraine said. "I protected Jeff in life and now I'm going to protect him in death."

* The Astle Gates, a lasting memorial to West Bromwich Albion's one and only "King" were unveiled at The Hawthorns by his widow on Friday, July 11, 2003.

Moseley's pied piper blows the final whistle

Saturday, January 25, 2003.

GREVILLE EDWARDS, Moseley Rugby Club's commercial manager and longest-serving employee, is busy slicing two dozen pork pies on a small wooden chopping board.

"They've won gold medals these pies," he said, carving enthusiastically. "I get them from Fladbury near Evesham. But you'll have to excuse me," he added. "I'm under pressure here." It's no wonder. This is a big afternoon. It's the "other" second city derby - yet it's a world away from Birmingham City versus Aston Villa.

Moseley are about to take on Birmingham & Solihull. Three decades ago, the fixture would have been inconceivable. Moseley were one of Britain's rugby elite. At their peak, in the 1970s, the team boasted seven internationals. Birmingham, meanwhile, were playing their matches on an open field. Today, they face each other head on in the National League first division and it's "The Bees" of Birmingham who reign supreme.

By contrast, Moseley Rugby Club, founded in 1873 (one year before Villa and two before Birmingham City), is a shadow of its former self. The club's temporary home is Birmingham University. While Edwards prepares his buffet, Dave Warren, the unpaid chief executive, is outside cleaning the portable toilet block. He's been here since 7.30am with his army of 20 willing volunteers. Without them, there would be no club at all. Warren took over the job just minutes before the first game of the season. Now he spends every spare second making sure Moseley survive.

"People ask me why I do it," Warren said, carrying his "trusty" mop and bucket. "Sometimes I don't know myself - it's hardly glamorous, is it?" he asked, peering down a toilet basin. "I must be bonkers," he added. "We have to do everything because we've got no money, no clubhouse, nothing. I carry on because I love the club. It's vital that this city has a leading rugby team. We've got a long way to go, but I still hope it can be us."

The sprawling campus of Birmingham's red brick university provides a picturesque setting for Moseley. A 335-foot clock tower, christened "Big Joe" after one of the city's forefathers Joseph Chamberlain, watches proudly over the ground. But it's no place for a big sporting fixture. As kick off approaches, the only cheers that can be heard are from a group of over-eager students having a friendly hockey knockabout on a nearby artificial pitch.

On the field, the Moseley players warm up as the club's antiquated public address system plays the Bee Gees hit *Tragedy*. Fewer than 600 spectators have turned out for the match - and not all of those have paid. Only a see-through builders mesh fence surrounds the ground, giving another 50 the chance to watch for nothing.

For the paying customers there is a temporary canvas grandstand. When the stand is full it seats 650. It's never full. A pair of green garden gazebos double for the two "turnstile" entrances. They are "guarded" by a pair of stout gentlemen perched precariously on fold-up fishing stools. Five replica shirts hang from the canvas ceiling of a small marquee which serves as the club shop. The teams change in a crumbling green prefab building 200 muddy yards from the pitch. Less than three miles down the road, Moseley's famous old home, The Reddings, lies derelict. The gates are padlocked and the buildings have been flattened.

Even commercial manager Edwards has called time on the club he loves. He is retiring today after almost 30 years. The pork pies, served with jars of Colman's English Mustard, were laid out in one of the student bars for his leaving bash. "It's a sad day. Moseley has been a way of life for me," he said.

Over the years, Edwards has raised thousands of pounds for Moseley. He was one of rugby's commercial pioneers in the days before the game's "big bang" when leagues were introduced, big money was invested and Moseley simply got left behind.

He was the first to introduce executive boxes at a rugby ground and Moseley were the first English club to have a significant sponsorship deal. He recalls the good old days all too readily. "Our glory decade was between 1972 and 1982," he said. In 1982 Moseley shared the John Player Cup with Gloucester after a 12-12 draw in the final at Twickenham. It was their last trophy. "Then the leagues came, we lost our Welsh fixtures, crowds suffered and things began to go wrong. Leaving The Reddings was the worst day's work we ever did."

The makeshift scoreboard at the far end of the ground reads Birmingham 22 Moseley 0 with only 30 minutes gone. "Another soft one given away," a fan standing in front of Fat Paddy's Catering Wagon yells. Replacement scrum half Charlie Millichip, grandson of former Football Association chairman Sir Bert, limbers up on the touchline. But even his presence doesn't help. It gets worse. By the final whistle Moseley have slumped to a 55-0 defeat. Like Greville's pork pies, they have been totally devoured. Only two league wins all season has left Moseley near the bottom of the table while Birmingham & Solihull have proved themselves again to be a club in the ascendancy.

Warren, who runs a small building firm in Highgate, mobilises his trusty band of volunteers. They have another two hours' work dismantling the ground before they can enjoy a drink with other club members. The last job is picking up the litter. It's a dirty job and not one that Warren's football counterpart Doug Ellis, the Aston Villa chairman, would relish.

"We should have a place in The Guinness Book of Records for the club that's made the most mistakes," Warren said, trying to figure out where it all went wrong for a club he played for, captained and then finally rescued from the brink of oblivion. "It's a soccer mad city and obviously I'm envious of the football clubs. But there are plenty of people in Birmingham who love rugby and I'm sure we've got a future."

He has reason to be optimistic. The city council has given Moseley a parcel of run-down land at Billesley Common. Already £12,000 has been raised by members to build a new clubhouse. "That's vital in getting the fans to return. At least they'll have somewhere to meet," Warren said. He hopes to be in the new home within 12 months.

"Until then, we'll keep at it and keep smiling. Playing alongside the best teams in the country again is out of the question at the moment," he said, stooping to pick up a discarded coffee cup. "But one way or another I'm optimistic they'll always be a Moseley Rugby Club."

* Still in a state of despondency having seen his side thrashed by their bitter local rivals, Moseley Chief Executive Dave Warren returned to the Birmingham University car park after his clean-up duties on January 25 to discover that his vehicle had been stolen. "It was a fitting end to a rather traumatic day," he said.

* Moseley's sad demise continues. They won only four of their 26 games last season and were relegated to the National League second division. They suffered a 36-25 home defeat to Exeter on the last day of the season. "Play

like that - and you'll soon be back," a visiting fan bellowed encouragingly as the players left the field dejected.

* Richard Protherough, captain and hooker, and lock Richard Stott immediately left the club to join Coventry. Moseley are still playing their home games at Birmingham University.

* Their future remains uncertain.

Five Star Villa

Tuesday, January 28, 2003.

ASTON VILLA achieved their first away win of the season in style when they demolished Middlesbrough 5-2 at the Riverside Stadium. Villa, who had previously scored only four goals on their travels, more than doubled that tally - and robbed their opponents of the Premiership's only unbeaten home record.

Darius Vassell scored twice, while Gareth Barry, Dion Dublin and Joey Gudjonsson, making his Villa debut, also got on the score-sheet.

Graham Taylor, the Aston Villa manager, said: "It's the end of an embarrassing record and we are very, very pleased about that."

Taylor singled out Gudjonsson for special praise. "I'm quite excited about Joey," he said. "He gives us an edge in midfield that we have not had all season. His age is right, the competitiveness about the boy is right - and he will get better."

Big Dave at home in the death business

Saturday, February 1, 2003.

IT'S A DULL WEDNESDAY MORNING. There's a hint of drizzle in the air as a small group of mourners shuffle solemnly through the wrought iron gates leading into Solihull Crematorium. Dave Latchford peers through the lodge-house window. "The thing is," he says, "you can't afford to make mistakes in the funeral industry. It's a bit like playing in goal."

Latchford should know. He spent 12 years playing in goal for Birmingham City before he was replaced by Gary Sprake.

Now his job is to look after the two cemeteries and three crematoriums in the borough of Solihull. He oversees more than 2,500 funerals every year. Death is his business - and business is always good.

Latchford, nicknamed "Big Dave", was born into a football-mad family in Kings Heath. He was one of four brothers, three of whom became professionals. Dave made 239 appearances for Birmingham City. Peter played in goal for Celtic after starting his career at West Bromwich Albion, while Bob, or as the family prefer, Robert, was a striker. He scored 263 goals for Birmingham City then moved to Everton in 1974 for a club record fee of £350,000.

The brother that got away was John. He could have been the best of the lot. As a promising full back he had trials with Aston Villa. "But being nine years older than the rest of us he wasn't encouraged to progress," Dave said. "It was different in those days. We'll never know how good he could have been.

Instead of football he took a toolmaker's apprenticeship," he added.

"Even so, it's unique having three brothers playing for different sides at the top level. I'm not sure it will happen again. As lads we cut up a few lawns and broke a few windows. Then, as professionals, we used to tread all over each other, kick lumps out of each other and even whack each other if we got the chance.

"I remember Robert making his home debut for Everton against Birmingham. The bugger scored against me! It was the goal that kick-started his Goodison career. Watching him celebrate, I looked to the heavens and thought, 'Oh lord no! Anybody but him.' That's what we were like."

The rivalry on the pitch was soon forgotten. "But we had some interesting Sunday lunches," Dave said with a smirk.

"One Saturday, Robert scored for Birmingham against Albion. Our young brother, Peter, was the Baggies' goalkeeper. My mother, Ada, was at the game and was horrified when Bob trod all over Peter's fingers to put the ball into the net. The day after she went berserk. I can hear her now, screaming 'don't you dare touch my little baby like that again.'"

Today, little baby Peter owns Bog Head farm in Ayrshire where he tends to his goats, sheep and horses. He's also part time goalkeeping coach for Heart of Midlothian. Robert is making a new life for himself in Austria after losing his first wife, Pat, through cancer five years ago. "We call him the Scarlet Pimpernel because we have not seen him for a while."

Dave is approaching his 25th year in the funeral trade. He became an undertaker by accident.

"I never, ever considered funeral directing as a career," he said. "But I had to do something - we didn't make a fortune playing football in those days. When my career ended my wife and I bought a small guesthouse in Weston-super-Mare, but to make ends meet I applied for a job as driver and bearer for local undertakers Pitman and Son. I'll never forget my first morning.

"There was a body found on the beach and I was sent with one of the lads to pick it up. When we arrived we found an abandoned car - inside was a man who'd just blown his brains out with a sawn off shotgun. There was a bottle of whisky by his side, blood everywhere in the vehicle and it was up to me to take this poor guy to the mortuary.

"I hadn't experienced anything like it before. I didn't know whether to run off screaming or stay put. I stayed. It was an extreme case but it was probably the best start I could have had. I couldn't face my sandwiches that dinnertime, though.

"It's never pleasant - but it's a job that has to be done," Latchford said. "The undertaker's most important tool is his caring attitude. How he conducts himself in front of the bereaved and how he handles them at such an emotional time."

Latchford and his family eventually moved back to Birmingham where he took up an undertaker's post with the Co-op in Nechells. "Once a Brummie, always a Brummie. Once a Bluenose, always a Bluenose," he said. "But now I've crossed over to the other side," he added quickly. That means instead of funeral directing, Latchford looks after the day-to-day running of cremations and burials at the five cemeteries and crematoriums in his patch. "Instead of bringing them in - I receive them."

He even lives in a cemetery, as the on-site caretaker of nearby Widney Manor. "At times the job gets difficult, of course it does. But I still have football as my release valve," Latchford said. He's a regular at St Andrew's and he's justifiably proud of a playing career that saw him represent his country at youth level, competing for the coveted goalkeeper's jersey with an "up-and-coming" Peter Shilton. Sir Alf Ramsey, "a true gentleman", was one of his Birmingham managers.

Today, with five granddaughters between the brothers, I suggest the Latchford football dynasty is over. Big Dave doesn't agree. "You never know," he said. "My son Ben has just completed a coaching course in America where women's football is very big. You've seen the Latchford boys - now here come the Latchford girls."

Big Dave laughs for a second and then composes himself. He's got a funeral to go to.

A TRUE BLUE SEND-OFF

How to die... the Birmingham City way

* To mark the arrival of Birmingham City into the Premiership, the Midland Co-op began a funeral service for Blues supporters who wanted to "show their loyalty and passion in the ultimate way". The 'True Blue' funeral was launched at the beginning of the season and, by February it was proving to be a big hit.

The "gold package" included a coffin lined in the blue and white of Birmingham City and "tastefully decorated" with the club's crest. A wreath, also made up in club colours, and an opportunity to scatter the deceased's ashes at St Andrew's (a ceremony that "may be witnessed by family and friends") was also thrown in. To complete the deal, a memorial brick would be placed to the left of the VIP entrance of the Kop Stand and a four line entry put in the club's official "Book of Remembrance."

Optional extras include a silk "Super Blues" flag which could be draped over the coffin, and a "memorial boulder" carrying the club's crest "to help overcome the starkness of a newly dug grave". The Co-op would even organise a wake in one of the executive boxes at

Birmingham's ground - as long as a match wasn't taking place at the same time.

"We're aiming at the kind of person who, whenever you hear the team's result, you can't help but think of them," a spokesman said. Supporters that were still alive and not even feeling ill were given the chance to reserve their cremation or burial by contacting a freephone number in the club's official match-day programme.

Boing the legend: live, uncensored and uncut

Saturday, February 8, 2003.

FIVE GREAT MYSTERIES OF OUR TIME: King Arthur and the Knights of the Round Table, Stonehenge, the Loch Ness Monster, the disappearance of Glenn Miller - and why West Bromwich Albion fans go boing, boing.

The latter has become a football oddity, one of the quirks of the Barclaycard Premiership. Those who study fan culture are bamboozled. Its origins are the cause of endless arguments in alehouses around the Midlands. It was recently the subject of a debate on BBC Radio 5 Live's *6-0-6* phone-in. The matter has even been raised on the floor of the House of Commons, courtesy of West Bromwich East MP and Baggies fanatic Tom Watson (nicknamed "the Honourable Member for West Bromwich Albion" by his Westminster colleagues).

Yet the inquiries of the football world have drawn a blank. Nobody can work out why those "odd folk in the Black Country" bounce up and down during games, at the drop of a hat. On *6-0-6*, I was named as "the man that started the craze".

That's not true. But I am one of the few who know the real story. And today, I'm going to reveal all. If you're sitting comfortably, then I'll begin.

The legend of the "boing" began in the summer of 1991 when a group of young Albion fans made an annual pilgrimage to the Costa Del Sol. There they discovered a song called *Poing* by the Rotterdam Transformation Source. The dance number, a big hit on the Continent, had a chorus that went

146

"Poing, Poing, Poing". It was similar to the noise made by Zebedee when he appeared from out of nowhere to inform his Magic Round-About chums that it was "time for bed.". You didn't dance to the tune. You bounced up and down.

On their return, our intrepid travellers prepared for the new football season. Things were grim at The Hawthorns. Albion had dropped into the third division for the first time. But the lads were desperate to add a little glamour to the visit of Exeter City on the first day of the season, so they cast their minds back to the sun-soaked beaches of Spain. Almost instinctively, they began to poing, poing up and down - all seven of them.

The "poing" was slow to catch on at first, but then came a dramatic turning point - on a filthy, rain soaked night at Preston North End's Deepdale ground. It was the first day of October, a date that might now go down in the annals of Albion history. The seven "poing" pioneers were there. They never missed - home or away. Distraught when their team went 2-0 down, they began a half-hearted poing, poing, mostly out of boredom but also in an attempt to keep warm on an unseasonably cold evening.

Tonight, however, there was magic in the air. Because of the exaggerated bounce of the ball on Preston's infamous plastic pitch - the poing, poing was subtly altered to a boing, boing. Out of the blue the bouncing slowly began to take off. Then, in another fateful twist, one of the seven added the words "Baggies, Baggies" to the "Boing, Boing". Now the chant and the bounce spread like wildfire among the travelling 500 fans in a crowd of 5,293. Soon the whole of the away section was at it. A legend was born.

As a radio reporter commentating on the game, I witnessed the first full-scale boing and wasted no time in announcing its arrival to armchair Albion fans waiting for the latest update back in the West Midlands. "Something special has happened at Deepdale tonight," I declared. That's why many people think Boyden and boinging go hand in hand.

Since then, a whole cottage industry has grown up in the Midlands, trading on the back of the boing. Sela, the Smethwick sweet company, has been making Boing Boing Ball Drops since the mid 1990s, Edgbaston's Ivy Bush Brewery did a steady trade in Boing Boing Brew for a number of years, while Keith Boxley, an award winning butcher from Wombourne, turned his hand to the Boing Boing Banger - the world's first navy blue sausage. It's still available on request.

Big H, The Birmingham Cowboy (Telford-based country singer Henry Conway), is just one recording artist who has tried to capture the phenomenon in song. His ditty, *The Legend of the Boing, Boing Man*, was released in 1995. For a while it bubbled just outside the top 100. Frankie Frossle was another pop-wannabe who set out for chart stardom with the more simply entitled, *Boing*.

The "mega boing" came when Albion beat Swansea City in a play-off semi-final at The Hawthorns in 1992. That evening the whole ground was transformed into a seething mass of bouncing bodies. It's never been bettered. The oldest boinger in town is Doris Wilton, 82. Before every Baggies home game she takes the 406 or the 451 bus from Great Barr to West Bromwich where she meets up with her friend, Madge, a mere novice boinger at 63. Doris has sat in the same part of the ground for more than 30 years. She never misses - and she still boings. "It keeps me young," she said. "It's better than any exercise video."

"Boing, boing" has even become an informal greeting among Albion fans.

Meanwhile, in an apartment in Rotterdam, Maurice Steenbergen, DJ, music producer and remixer, sits twiddling with his turntables. He created the Rotterdam Transformation Source, and the dance hit *Poing* when he was just 19-years-old. He's the real "boing master". He knows it and he's proud of the way he's enhanced the lives of thousands of football fans. "I'm truly honoured," he said. "In fact, I'd like to take this opportunity to offer the club an exclusive live performance at their stadium. I'm also planning a new anthem, *The Baggies will knock you out.*"

In time, Feyenoord football fan Maurice, who's currently producing the music for a Playboy Magazine commercial, could become as much a part of Black Country folklore as boxer William Perry, "The Tipton Slasher" or Netherton's "Jumping Joe Darby", the man who could leap over a canal from a standing start.

That's the definitive explanation. Don't let anyone ever tell you different. At West Ham United they blow bubbles, Birmingham City supporters sing *Keep Right on to the End of the Road* - and Albion fans boing, boing. That's the way it is. And that's the way it will always be.

And it's all thanks to the magnificent seven, a plastic football pitch - and a Dutchman.

Tuesday, July 15, 2003.

WEST BROMWICH ALBION'S boing, boing song was officially labelled football's weirdest chant in a survey compiled by Thomson - the package holiday specialist. Celery, a pleasant ditty performed by Chelsea supporters came a close number two in the weird soccer song top-ten, followed by the West Ham United anthem I'm Forever Blowing Bubbles.

Saturday, September 12, 1903.

SO, WHY ARE ALBION nicknamed The Baggies? Is it because they were the last football team to change to the fashionable shortened playing shorts? Was it something to do with the turnstile operators at The Hawthorns strolling past the main stand during a Saturday afternoon game, on route to the cashier's office, carrying heavy blue bags bulging with entrance fee money?

No, is the answer to both. Here, again, is the precise, proper and definitive explanation. Cut it out and keep it in your breast pocket. If anybody asks again, you'll have the true facts at your fingertips.

Originally, Albion were known as The Throstles. Then, on Saturday, September 12, 1903, a group of iron foundry workers from the Black Country decided to walk across the Birmingham boundary to watch their team play at Villa Park. It was a long trek and a great adventure for the two-dozen or so that dared to make the trip. Having just finished a gruelling 12 hour shift, our heroes were still decked out in their working clothes, industrial boots and heavy grey moleskin trousers that were held up by thick leather belts instead of the more traditional braces. As they spent most of their working day on their knees, the trousers - that already had a baggy look to them because of the lack of braces - were also covered with squares of "duck" material, known as "bag patches" which had been expertly sewn on by the women of the households to cover the holes.

News of Albion's "great march" to Villa spread quickly among football supporters in the Midlands, and many home fans gathered on the border to "welcome" those queer folk from the Black Country into their manor. They taunted them gently with cries of "Here come the bag men", referring to the men's baggy trousers that were also covered in bag patches. During the 1903-04 season, the "bag men" became local celebrities, and the cry was altered to, "Here come the Baggies".

Albion's travelling martyrs, thrilled by their notoriety, began calling themselves "The Baggies" and the name soon became linked to the club itself. The nickname made its first appearance in the club's matchday programme during the 1905-06 season.

From humble beginnings, another football legend had been born.

* Albion lost that historical 1903 fixture 3-1 and were relegated from the division at the end of the season.

* Now, about Glenn Miller....

Hell-raiser Tindall
discovers heaven in Jesus

Saturday, February 15, 2003.

BROMSGROVE HIGH STREET is slow to wake up. A flower seller busily arranges his Valentine bouquets under a frosty canopy. A handful of hardy shoppers scurry from stall to stall, stooping to shelter from the icy winds. Beneath the statue of poet A.E. Housman, the town's most famous son, a small man reaches inside a black bag. He pulls out a microphone and begins to preach.

"Good morning, everybody," Mike Tindall, the former Aston Villa wing-half says. "I'm here to talk to you about Jesus."

Nobody is listening. The don't want to know. Tindall is unperturbed. Over the next two hours he'll be physically harassed by some, verbally abused by many and ridiculed by all. He'll turn the other cheek. "I'm a disciple of Jesus," he says. "I'm his messenger. I'd happily preach seven days a week, 24 hours a day, 365 days a year. Anywhere in the world."

Tindall, 62 but looking ten years younger, was a football playboy of the late 1950s and early 1960s. He played in the same England youth team as Bobby Moore. Black and white pictures of him in action hang in the hallway of his home, yet his transformation from England squad to God squad has been dramatic.

"I was the world's worst. The original Jack the Lad," he said. "If Jesus can save me, he can save anybody. I had the most diabolical mouth, I lived in the nightclubs of Birmingham and did everything a Christian shouldn't. I'd booked a front-row seat in the theatre of Hell."

After 16 years as a professional footballer, Tindall's taste for the high life continued when he became landlord of the Coach and Horses pub in Bromsgrove. "I was making a fortune. A lot of customers were Villa fans and they loved to come and talk football. Then, all of a sudden, trade dropped," he said. "It was like somebody was standing outside telling punters not to come in." That was the start of his "new beginning". Upset and depressed, he decided to join Thora, his wife, at church one Sunday morning. It was February 1, 1987 - a day he'll never forget.

"I had never been to church before so I decided to sit at the back," he said, his face now full of emotion. "Suddenly I looked up and through the eyes of faith I saw Jesus. He said, 'Do not fear because I am with you. I have put my blessing on you and I will smooth the way before you. My love for you is more powerful than all of your weaknesses.'

"He asked me to go and tell the world about him. I was transformed in a second. Jesus spoke to my heart that day. It was the greatest moment of my life."

Tindall moved out of the pub business with hardly a penny to his name. He has "lived off his faith", with no regular income for the last 14 years. "I preach because that's what I've been called to do," he said. "At first, everyone thought I'd gone raving mad - even my family disowned me. I suppose their reaction was acceptable because they were witnessing such an immediate and dramatic change in me. Most people come to know Jesus over a period of time - I crashed into him head-on at 500mph. Since then I've been preaching non-stop. I've been physically attacked, spat at and I'm verbally abused all the time, but it doesn't bother me. I never get scared. The abuse is part of the cost of being a disciple of Christ.

"Most Christians won't pay that price. Jesus paid with his life," he said.

"Football prepared me for what was to come. If you can cope with 60,000 people calling you names when you're on the pitch, you can stand anything. I have seen grown men crying in the dressing-room, not wanting to go out for the second half because it was too hard. They would hide on the field. I was completely different. I used to blow kisses to the crowd if I was getting barracked."

As a boy, playing for Villa was Tindall's only ambition. He would hammer a leather football against the wall of his Acocks Green home for hours in pursuit of his dream. Eventually, he made the Villa number four shirt his own, becoming a vital member of the club's much admired "Mercer's Minors" team of the early 1960s. The fairytale ended, however, when he broke his leg at Tottenham Hotspur in November 1964. Jimmy Greaves helped to carry him off the field. Although he later joined Walsall, Tindall never fully recovered from the injury.

"It was a privilege to play football. It gave me some wonderful memories," he said. "All my dreams were fulfilled. I was earning £60 a week when a pint of beer cost a shilling. I was the designer king - made-to-measure suits, Italian shoes, everything. I travelled the world and played against some of the greats. But I realise now that it was all garbage compared to my life with Jesus. These days, I'm on another planet.

"David Beckham can earn all the money in the world, but one day he'll die and there are no favourites in heaven. All of today's players with their big cars and big houses will ultimately stand before Jesus - and their possessions are going to count for nothing."

Supported by his local church, Tindall travels the world preaching. He returned recently from a seven-week stint in Africa.

"While I was there, I saw the blind receive their sight, the lame walk and the sick healed through prayer," he said. "There was a guy on crutches. I prayed for him in the name of Jesus and he threw his crutches away. We prayed for a woman who was blind from birth and she began to regain her sight. It happened because they had faith. I'm not worshipping a dead religious leader. He's alive. He is here now. Wherever I go He's with me."

Tindall reached out to touch my shoulder. "The only thing that will keep you out of heaven is rejecting Jesus," he said. For a few seconds he prayed on my behalf. "There. You've repented your sins," he added calmly. "Now you'll go to heaven."

* *Mark Landreth-Smith, via email, writes: "Thank you for your piece on Saturday. I found it challenging, refreshing and shocking all in one. I am press officer for 'Newfrontiers' - a family of over 30 so-called new churches, lead by Terry Virgo."*

* *David Oliver, via email, writes: "I was much encouraged by your article and suggest that a television documentary is made of Mike Tindall's life and Christ's work in him. I pray that his prayer for you will be taken on by you, and that you will be in heaven because of Christ's work in you."*

* *Peter Lockley, via email, writes: "I've experienced something of Jesus's healing power myself and found Mike Tindall's conversion to Christianity very interesting."*

Starr answers SOS to raise Phoenix's profile

Saturday, February 22, 2003.

EDWIN STARR is a Motown legend. In 1970, his seminal single, *War*, sold more than 3 million copies, while another classic - the celebrated *Stop her On Sight (SOS)* was a Top 40 hit twice over in the mid-1960s. His showbiz friends include Michael Jackson and Liza Minnelli. Revered in all four corners of the globe as the "soul master", he's been an inspiration to generations of performers from Marvin Gaye to Bruce Springsteen.

Yet on Sunday lunchtimes, you can find him ankle-deep in mud, frozen to the core and screaming himself hoarse watching "his football team" at the Co-op Sports Ground in Yardley, Birmingham.

Born Charles Hatcher in Nashville, yet a West Midlands resident since 1983, Starr sponsors Phoenix Rangers under-14s in the third division of the Central Warwickshire League. The boys have his name emblazoned across their blue and yellow shirts. They look up to him. He's their idol - even though most of them were born 24 years *after* he exploded on to the British pop scene in 1966.

Starr, who has just been voted the leading live act ever by northern soul aficionados, cuts an intense, animated figure when he is watching Rangers play. These are humble surroundings in the shadow of Yardley Old Church, yet he's lost in his own world. He patrols the touchline like a wild animal stalking its prey. His unmistakable American "rough soul shout" is used to full effect when encouraging his lads.

"It's an honour to be supporting these kids," he said. "They're a wonderful group of teenagers. Hard working and honest. We've got some good players and the team spirit is fantastic. I come and cheer them on whenever I can. If they see me as an inspiration, then that makes me very happy. People who are trying to achieve in life need something and someone to look up to.

"It's all about putting something back," Starr, who lives in a 16th century manor house in Polesworth, near Tamworth, added. "I'm repaying the people of the West Midlands who have been so wonderful to me since I first came to Britain. They took me to their hearts straight away and made me feel so welcome. This area is now very much my home. It's where I'm most comfortable."

Ian Causon, the Phoenix Rangers manager and son of Bill Causon, the former West Bromwich Albion centre half, invited Starr to come and see the boys four years ago. "His guitar player is my old school friend," he explained. "I cheekily asked him if Edwin would be interested in helping the lads and the reply came back that he would love to. He had no hesitation. Now, he is a great supporter - although he does get rather vocal when he's watching."

He needs to be. Rangers are having a tough time. They are second from bottom of the league having lost Drew Maclean, their star player and grandson of toothy *Crackerjack* comedian Don, to the game of rugby at the start of the season. Tomorrow they take on high-flying Sporting FC at home. The manager recognises that it's going to be a difficult match - and a long, hard season.

But Causon knows all about life at the wrong end of the table. Despite being brought up in an Albion-dominated family, he is a Birmingham City fanatic. His most prized possession is his season ticket for the Tilton Stand. As well as his football, he's also becoming a regular on the soul circuit. "Edwin makes sure I go to his concerts when he's in the Midlands," he said. "He introduces me to friends as his 'football manager'. I've met Jimmy James of the Vagabonds and Martha Reeves of the Vandellas.

"I'd like to get Edwin to perform in our club hut, but by the time he'd set up with his 14 piece band there would be no room for an audience."

Sport has been a part of Edwin Starr's life since he was a young lad growing up in Cleveland. He excelled at track and field before playing American football as a receiver. Now he rates the "English game" as his one of his great passions - and he, too, is an ardent Birmingham City fan. "I would say without reservation that they are my favourite professional team," he said. "The club's owner, David Sullivan, insists he is my number one fan. His favourite record of all time is SOS."

Starr, whose smash hit H.A.P.P.Y R.A.D.I.O is in the Music Hall of Fame, was guest of honour and top of the bill at Birmingham's promotion party last season. Now the northern soul perennial who describes himself as music's "great survivor" is backing Blues to stave off the threat of relegation. He's confident that, under Steve Bruce, his adopted team will not only survive, but thrive. "Football is the same as the music business," he said. "When you've dragged yourself up by the bootstraps to sample life at the top, you'll give anything and everything in the world to stay there. I'm confident Blues will be in the Premiership next season."

As well as performing for footballers, Starr sang to a worldwide audience before Frank Bruno's world heavyweight boxing bout with Oliver McCall at Wembley Stadium. In April, he will fly to Los Angeles to attend the first anniversary party of Liza Minnelli and David Gest. He serenaded the couple at their wedding, where he was reunited with Michael Jackson, his friend for more than 35 years.

BRUM'S THE WORD

Recently, he has been in demand to talk about that friendship - and he's always happy to do so. "Michael is many different things to many different people," said Starr, who remembers their first meeting at the Apollo Theatre in New York. Jackson was just 8-years-old. "He is very misunderstood, very naive. Almost too honest for his own good," Starr added.

"He doesn't understand diplomacy - he would not know how to skate around an awkward situation. He's never had to because of his fame, his money and the protection his lifestyle has given him. In many ways he's still the child I met all those years ago."

* This was Edwin Starr's last national newspaper interview. He died of a heart attack at his home on Wednesday, April 2, 2003.

Leading the tributes, 70s rock star Suzi Quatro, told me: "He was the very best. There was nobody better on stage and he was the nicest man you could ever wish to meet. We had been very close friends for many years and I'm just stunned by the news."

Michael Jackson added: "As Edwin's legendary song, 25 Miles, states, 'he's gonna keep walking forever'. He will always be remembered."

Phoenix Rangers changed their name for the start of the current season. They are now called Edwin Starr FC, in tribute to their sponsor, their mentor and their best mate. Ian Causon, still the team's manager, said: "I was talking to Edwin two hours before he died. He had just agreed to do a charity concert for "his lads". That's the sort of man he was, fantastic with the boys and a wonderful example to us all. We still miss him very much. Sundays are not the same without him bellowing at us from the touchline."

BRUM'S THE WORD

Edwin Starr was a true soul master to the rich and famous. To his adopted family in the West Midlands - he was a true friend.

Wolves loyalist Bull happy to suffer for his art

Saturday, March 1, 2003.

BASIL THE SECURITY MAN is beaming. "There's a legend waiting for you in the green room," he says.

The green room he's talking about is on the first floor of Birmingham's BBC headquarters at Pebble Mill. Opened in 1971, the building is now a sad old lady, far removed from the glittering princess that pioneered some of the finest television shows of its day and is still the home of *The Archers*, Britain's longest-running soap opera. Next year the complex will be abandoned forever as the BBC turns its back on Edgbaston for a new base in the regenerated city centre - it will be the end of a broadcasting era.

The legend in the green room is Steve Bull MBE, the former Wolverhampton Wanderers and England forward. As a guest on a local radio programme, he too is about to reflect on the end of an era. Bull, 38 this month, still has the look of a goal scorer. He's tanned, lean and as fit as he's ever been. He sits reading the sports section of the *Birmingham Evening Mail*, gently sipping coffee out of a brown plastic cup. In the not too distant past, his name would have graced its pages night after night.

But his time has gone - the game has moved on.

Bull now spends his days as an entertainer. His one-man show plays to packed houses at venues such as the Wednesfield Social Club and the Horse and Jockey Pub in Coseley. He is also in demand on the after-dinner speaking circuit. He yearns to be involved in football management but his big break is yet to come.

Sold to Wolverhampton Wanderers by Ron Saunders, the West Bromwich Albion manager, in 1986 ("He told me my first touch wasn't good enough to make it in professional football"), Bull soon became a Black Country hero. He made his name as a prolific goalscorer, but turned down a number of high-profile moves, preferring to stay at Molineux for 16 years. He was the last of football's "loyal servants". He doesn't think the game will ever see his type again.

"I was gold and black through and through," he said. "I could have moved for the glamour and the money but that was never a consideration. I loved the club. I played from the heart - I was always hungry for Wolves." Bull's 306th and final league goal, against Bury on September 26, 1998, has been captured on canvas by Stourbridge artist Geoff Tristram. The limited edition oil painting is called *The End of an Era.*

Tentatively, I suggest that he had made a mistake sticking with one club for so long. Bull bowed his head, thought for a second and finally admitted: "You're right." He answered with a sigh as if a nagging burden had been removed from his chest. "I certainly haven't been rewarded for my loyalty. I would encourage today's players to make a move or two. That must sound strange coming from a man who always stayed put but it's how I feel," he said.

Steve Bull's frustrations have been simmering for a while. It's no wonder they've finally spilled out. His dream is to manage Wolverhampton Wanderers. But he's had no "leg-up" from the club he worships and that's been a bitter pill to swallow. "I thought Wolves might have helped me with my ambition to coach. They haven't and, believe me, that hurts deeply," he said.

Over the past few months he has been working for an "A level" coaching badge. It's been a hard slog, but now Bull's had to put his books away because he can't complete the course unless he gets a job working with a team. Professional or semi-professional. He's beginning to get desperate. "I miss the game more and more every day," he said. "It's my priority now to work for a club. Any club. I'm prepared to do anything - as long as it's not putting the nets up."

Bull is used to fighting his way to the top. His love affair with the game began as a young boy, but he worked in a builder's yard, at a bed factory and finally as a warehouseman before an Albion scout spotted him playing for Tipton Town and asked him, at the age of 19, to join the Baggies under-14s squad.

When Saunders released him, he was handed a lifeline by Wolves. "It took me just four minutes to sign on the dotted line," he said. "I had nothing to lose." Even though he supported Liverpool as a boy, he was soon to fall head over heels in love with his new club. He still attends Wolves games home and away. Next weekend he'll be at Southampton as his team attempt to reach the semi-finals of the FA Cup. "I'm convinced we'll be going to Cardiff this season," he said. "If not in the Cup then in the play-off finals."

Bull appeared in the 1998 FA Cup semi-final with Wolves who were beaten by Arsenal at Villa Park. He never played at the top level for the club, but won 13 caps for England, scoring a goal on his debut against Scotland at Hampden Park in May 1989. "I remember going on as substitute for John Fashanu," he said. "He gave me a high five in passing and said, 'Good luck Dave'." The image of that goal is also going to be captured in oils.

So, too, will be his meeting with the Queen on the day he was appointed MBE. "I'll never forget that moment," he said.

"Her Majesty looked straight at me; she seemed to have a quizzical stare on her face. After a few seconds, she shook her head in disbelief and mumbled, 'I can't believe you once played for the Baggies'."

BRUM'S THE WORD

* *Wolverhampton Wanderers missed out on an FA Cup Final appearance in Cardiff when they were beaten 2-0 by Southampton in the quarter-finals at St Mary's Stadium. But, as predicted by Steve Bull, the club eventually managed to enjoy a big day out at the Millennium Stadium as finalists in the first division play-offs.*

* *Steve Bull is still looking for his first coaching job in football.*

Double, double woofle dust!

Monday, March 3, 2003.

BIRMINGHAM CITY completed their first second city derby double in 26 years when they beat bitter rivals Aston Villa 2-0 on a manic Monday night at Villa Park. The Midlands' "showpiece occasion" degenerated into a poisonous affair, described by one national newspaper as a "ferocious blur of a match" played out amidst "violent skirmishes off the field, a flurry of red cards on the pitch and the purring menace of police helicopters hovering above".

Goals by Stan Lazaridis and substitute Geoff Horsfield, who took advantage of another Peter Enckelman blunder, gave Blues victory, although Villa ended the match with nine men after Dion Dublin and Joey Gudjonsson were shown red cards. Dublin's head-butt on Welsh international Robbie Savage provoked a near riot from fans in the Doug Ellis stand.

Savage, the consummate performer, controlled the evening's "entertainment" from start to finish, but was finally substituted for "his own good" after being confronted by an angry home fan who had the neck to stage a one-man pitch invasion.

For some supporters, the date, Monday, March 3rd, 2003, will go down as a "tipping point" in West Midlands' football; when Birmingham City began to emerge from out of the shadows to take their place as the region's biggest and most successful club.

BRUM'S THE WORD

Steve Bruce, the Birmingham manager, paid tribute to his players after the game for the way they conducted themselves. Graham Taylor, his raging Villa counter-part, stormed away from an after-match televised press conference, but later composed himself to admit, "We have let a lot of people down in terms of our performance and lack of discipline. The game was not an advert for the type of football or atmosphere that I feel is right."

Doug Ellis, the Aston Villa chairman, insisted: "There is no doubt in my mind that we have a rewarding future in front of us with Graham Taylor in charge."

* Graham Taylor, the Aston Villa manager, resigned on Wednesday, May 14, 2003, three days after the end of the football season.

Shrove Tuesday

Tuesday, March 4, 2003.

IT'S THE MORNING AFTER the night before. Emotions are running high across the Midlands. Aston Villa fan Jim Lewis scours the morning papers. He shakes his head in disbelief. "It's depressing and frustrating," he said with a sigh. "Nobody applauded louder than me when Birmingham City got promoted. I wanted all of our teams in the top division. But how can any true fan be proud of what went on last night?" He thinks again. "And Graham Taylor?" he adds. "It makes you wonder if he's capable of motivating or controlling his team. Pathetic. I'm deeply disappointed."

Within a second, Jim's mood takes a turn. He picks up another paper. "Look," he said. "They reckon my horse is the most perfect steeplechaser ever." Now he's in dreamland. The upset of last night's Birmingham derby is beginning to subside. In the bathroom, his wife Val is half way up a stepladder. She's having to tread carefully in her fluffy pink slippers. "It's all right," Jim said, reassuringly. "I've sent her into the loft. That's where we keep the Cheltenham Gold Cup."

It's a peculiar, topsy-turvy morning in the Lewis house.

Racehorses and Aston Villa are Jim's two great passions. Today he doesn't know whether to laugh or cry. As owner of Best Mate, the Gold Cup winner last year, he's full of excitement and busy making final preparations for next week's Cheltenham Festival - the highlight of his sporting year. His racing colours are the claret and blue stripes of Villa's 1957 FA Cup-winning shirt. Anybody accompanying him in the paddock must wear a Villa scarf. "Those are the strict rules," he said.

His love for Villa began as a nine-year-old, when he hitched a lift on the back of a coal wagon from Ward End Road to Villa Park. He idolised Frank Broome in the 1940s and got his mother to cut out a number seven from an old pair of her bloomers so he could have it sewn onto the back of his shirt. "Whenever we played as kids in Ward End Park, I was Frankie Broom," Jim, who went on to play inside forward for Dudley Town, said. It's no wonder that today he's torn between agony and ecstasy.

"My first game watching Villa was against Birmingham. I was lifted over the turnstiles by my neighbour Alfie Aston. Within no time I was a die hard fan," Jim said, remembering his early days on the Witton terrace. "Later on, Val and I had season tickets for both West Bromwich Albion and Villa. A lot of people did in those days because they played at home on different weekends." Val, his childhood sweetheart and wife of 46 years, has emerged from the loft with the Gold Cup. It's draped in claret and blue ribbons.

"This," he said, pointing proudly at the trophy, "is the culmination of a wild dream. Nobody in their right mind would have thought a working-class kid from Ward End Road would grow up to own the Gold Cup-winning horse. I was invited to Villa as a special guest when we won it and I did my own lap of honour. I had never been on the pitch before and it was a tremendous thrill. I remember thinking, 'I'm 68 years old and I'm running around Villa Park like a teenager waving a cup!' Ridiculous."

Jim's love for horses began at the same time as his passion for Villa. While delivering newspapers to Birmingham's now-defunct Bromford Bridge course, he would read the racing pages from top to bottom and carefully remember the tips. "I began betting when I was about ten-years-old," he said. "Then, when I was 16, I stood with Val on Bromford Bank and promised I would buy her a racehorse one day."

After making his money importing furniture from South Africa and Brazil, Jim stayed true to his word and bought Pearl Prospect to celebrate their pearl wedding anniversary. Right on cue, Val has emerged from the loft. Carefully she is carrying the King George VI Chase trophy into the room. Best Mate won that at Kempton Park on Boxing Day.

"If he wins at Cheltenham he'll be the first horse to retain the Gold Cup since L'Escargot in 1971. That's a tremendous achievement," Jim said. "He won last year at the age of seven with such dignity and style. I'm starting to think he is the most perfect horse ever."

Jim has five horses running in the festival, including Edredon Bleu, who won the Queen Mother Champion Chase in 1999. "I was the last person to receive the trophy from Her Majesty. She was 100 years old," Jim said, pointing to the picture. It's one of hundreds that hang in every room of his home, competing for space with the Villa flags, signed footballs - and cuddly black cats for luck.

"When I arrive at Cheltenham I can feel myself starting to tremble in anticipation. I watch every race from the same spot on the lawn in front of the grandstand," he said. "It's where I stood when Nakir became my first Cheltenham winner in 1994. It's probably the worst view on the course but, being from a poor background I'm very superstitious," he said.

He hates green. Loves the number 15 and has a special black cat that he takes to every race meeting. It's a small, plastic animal crudely covered in cheap black suede. It was a 1960s fairground gift that is long since past its prime. Around its neck, there's a claret and blue ribbon.

Val reappears from the loft again. She's brought Jim's "Oscar". He was voted leading owner of 2002 by the Racehorse Owners' Association. It's one of his proudest achievements but thoroughly deserved. As well as the greatest, he's also the nicest - and surely the most humble.

"I often wonder how much luckier I can get," Jim said. "But then, in life I've always tried to find a reason to be hopeful - even when I was struggling to make ends meet as a bed salesman at Slumberland. If you don't harbour dreams, you've got nothing to look forward to. I always say: 'Never look back unless you can smile and never look forward unless you can dream.'"

This week, more than any other, Villa fans would do well to take heed.

Cheltenham Gold Cup day

Thursday, March 13, 2003.

BEST MATE completed an historic double when he cruised to his second Cheltenham Gold Cup in succession. The 13-8 favourite destroyed the rest of the field - steeplechasing's crème de la crème - winning by 10 lengths from 33-1 outsider Truckers Tavern who came second, and Harbour Pilot (40-1) third. Roared on by a massive Prestbury Park crowd, horse racing's new hero took control after jumping the third-last fence and was never in danger as he strode clear to land the £203,000 first prize in magnificent style.

Jim Lewis, clearly overcome with emotion after the race, accepted the Gold Cup from The Queen, on her first visit to the meeting in 50 years. "This," he said, stroking horse racing's most prestigious trophy with his left hand, "is going straight back into the loft."

Lewis, complete with Villa scarf and lucky black cat, added: "I've got a heartbeat going so fast that I could beat eggs. History has been made - I cannot believe it. My trainer, Henrietta Knight, is a weaver of dreams."

One Irish punter has laid a £25,000 cash bet on Best Mate completing his Gold Cup hat-trick in March 2004. Bookmakers are currently quoting the horse at 7-4 favourite for the race. Experts reckon that Best Mate is now officially, "the most perfect steeplechaser in history".

Another Blues full house?
Mum's the word

Saturday, March 15, 2003.

IT IS MONDAY LUNCHTIME and St Andrew's is a hive of activity. A convoy of Ring and Ride buses arrives outside the Trevor Francis Suite. Inside, Ron Caswell, a Birmingham City season ticket-holder turned bingo-caller ("I'm 80 in August, you know") is testing his microphone. A steady stream of pensioners files quietly into the room. One by one they pay homage to a pair of distinguished ladies in the corner. Welcome to the Birmingham City Senior Citizens Club - probably the most unique football gathering of its kind in the world.

The distinguished ladies are 86-year-old Thelma Sullivan, mother of David, the club president, and 88-year-old Rosie Gold, whose sons, David and Ralph are Blues chairman and director respectively. The three men are joint owners of the club - they are also notorious for their involvement in the pornographic industry. Their charming mothers run the Monday get-together, which means a weekly trip from London to play bingo with Birmingham's more elderly supporters.

One old-timer has "We 8 Villa" displayed proudly on the back of his Birmingham shirt. "It's amazing, isn't it?" he says, surveying the room. "Where else in football would you find a pensioners' club like this, run by the owners' mums? They're golden, these ladies," he added, giving Rosie a peck. "They're royalty to us."

Rosie, 89 in July, laps up the attention. "I adore looking after elderly people," she said. "What goes on here is just as important as the football. It gives the old folk a lot of pleasure - for some it's their only outing of the week." She adjusts her silk scarf. "This club has become my life. I love the people, and it seems they love me."

It's eyes down, look in. Ron calls the first game, and he's got a good line in bingo patter. ("Two and six, half a crown.... Take to the floor, number four..." Seven and six, was she worth it?") A nervy hush descends on the room. With each full house worth £10, it's a serious business.

Between games, the two mothers have time to talk about their sons. "It was David Sullivan - my boy, who pressed the button here," Thelma said, glowing with pride. "The club was in a hell of a state. It was in the throes of folding. He had a lot of courage," she stops to think. "But I do love my football," she said, bending to whisper with a mischievous grin. "David bought me Sky before Christmas so I can watch it all now. Rosie and me never miss a home game. They sit us in the directors' box, just behind the boys."

"My two are angels," Rosie Gold adds. "When they bought the club I was so proud. I never thought it would happen. Who would've guessed that I would get to meet people like Karren Brady? It's wonderful. And I want for nothing. I've never had a wardrobe like the one I've got now in all my life!"

Thirty years ago, Rosie found that she had lung cancer and was given just months to live. "I remember the boys around my bed with flowers. I was on my last legs," she said. "But I fought back and I've never had a day's illness since - that's my proudest boast. I don't want to die either. I'm enjoying myself too much."

Ralph and David Gold were brought up in the shadows of West Ham United's ground in London's tough East End. It was a struggle for Rosie. "We had absolutely nothing," she said. "I had to work long hours on the buses, then come home and make meals out of anything I could lay my hands on. Their father was a womaniser and a gambler. He'd spend money as fast as I could earn it." Eventually, she and the boys set up a stall "flogging buttons while the old man was inside". Later they'd sell "job-lot comics" at three for a shilling. It was the humble beginnings of what became a publishing empire.

David had trials for West Ham but his father demanded that he turned down a career in the game to keep his trade as a bricklayer. "I don't think he's ever forgiven him," Rosie said. "But he got his way in the end, being involved with football at the highest level." She nudges me gently in the arm. "He tells the press he's 61, but he's not. He's 66. I should know," she giggles like a schoolgirl. But then, she still feels like one. "I go to the gym every week - 20 minutes on the treadmill and half an hour on the bike. Then, I'm out at bingo almost every night. I'm a right little Mary-Anne." She prods me again. "Mind you, I'm an attractive old bird for nearly 90. God's been good to me."

Rosie worked in her own greetings card shop until she was 82 when David suggested she retired in order to run the Birmingham City Senior Citizens Club. She keeps records of every member in her black briefcase. Each one pays £3 a year for the privilege of a weekly bingo session, a Christmas party and "the occasional outing". Lunchtime has flown. Ron's called his last game, but on their way out, each member waits in turn to steal a kiss from the two heroines. Some pass on gifts, others hand over newspaper cuttings featuring Rosie and Thelma's boys.

"We love reading about Birmingham City," Rosie said. "I'll collect anything on Robbie Savage. He's my favourite - I love watching him play. He's such a nice young man. He's got a heart of gold, you know."

Thelma Sullivan shows me her handbag. It was a gift from David and has a colour picture of himself and his two boys printed on the front and back. "I'm thrilled to bits with all of this," she said. "Every day is like a holiday. Rosie and me know what it's like to be poor, but I always knew David would do well. He told me he'd make £500 by the time he was 18. I told him he was talking codswallop, but he did it. Then he spent the lot watching Newport County play.

"But he's a wonderful lad - rings me every morning to make sure I'm all right," she said. "Wait till I tell him I'm going to be in the newspapers."

Rosie and Thelma are about to return to London. The car is waiting. St Andrew's is quiet again. "Make sure you give us a good write-up," Rosie says, gently raising her walking stick as the chauffeur covers her legs with a tartan blanket. "We've got Kevin Keegan's lot next and we need another win."Thelma intervenes. "Don't worry, we're going to stay up for sure," she said reassuringly. "After all, we're the lucky mascots."

Saying goodbye
to the world

Monday, March 17, 2003.

BIRMINGHAM WAVES a fond farewell to 500 competitors from more than 140 countries as the curtain falls on the World Indoor Athletics Championships, which have been taking place at the city's National Indoor Arena over the weekend.

The event, the biggest of its kind held in Britain since the 1948 Olympics, was described as "magical" by David Moorcroft, the United Kingdom's head of athletics. "I'm absolutely delighted," he said. "The atmosphere has been great, the athletes are happy and the organisation has been excellent. We, and Birmingham, have delivered."

Many visitors, including Bill Clinton, the former American President, added their weight behind Birmingham's bid to become the European Capital of Culture 2008. "It's an extraordinary jewel of a city," Clinton said.

But four-year-old William Parkinson got a little confused. Attending his first athletics meeting, he said: "I really want Colin Jackson to win gold. But David Beckham is my favourite."

* Birmingham failed in its bid to become the European Capital of Culture 2008. The honour was, instead, given to Liverpool.

Chinn views Villa as his latest deserving cause

Saturday, March 22, 2003.

PROFESSOR CARL CHINN is A man of the people. He is ferociously proud of his city - it's a place he will always protect and defend. When he speaks about the West Midlands, passion flows through every vein in his body. To some he is the fighter who helped save the Rover car plant from collapse three years ago. For others he is a trusted voice in an often ridiculed city.

Now, he's being spoken of as a potential knight in shining armour for another famous Birmingham institution - Aston Villa Football Club. It's a mountain he's finally ready to start climbing.

Chinn's study tells the story of his life. Books on Joseph Chamberlain, the Victorian cabinet minister and father of a future Prime Minister, tussle for space alongside the biographies of George Cadbury and Lord Denis Howell - all great Brummies. One shelf houses his "Villa collection". There's a picture of his beloved grandmother, Lilly, with her arms around her football hero, Eric Houghton. Squeezed into the corner of the room, a model vintage truck has the words "Carl Chinn. Historian. Birmingham" hand-painted on the side. The words sum him up perfectly.

Chinn, a professor of community history at Birmingham University, was born a Villa fan. His love affair with the club began when his mother, Sylvia, held him in front of the window to watch the 1957 FA Cup winning team parade past The Albion pub in Aston. He was eight months old. Buck, his father, an illegal bookmaker from Sparkbrook who is now chairman of the club's Shareholders Association, and Lilly, who stood on the Holte End until she was 74, kept his passion alive. "The first fight I ever saw at Villa Park involved my Nan," Chinn said. "She threw a wicked right hook and downed an away supporter who tried to pinch my brother's woolly hat. She was only four feet 11, but she was a tough Aston girl.

Chinn, who watched Villa lose 6-2 to Chelsea on his first visit to Villa Park, added: "I was thoroughly engrossed from a small child. If we were defeated I used to take it personally. It was my fault. I'd hung my scarf up wrong or hadn't said my prayers correctly. I loved Tommy Docherty. I remember meeting the great man on the steps of the then beautiful Trinity Road Stand. I froze with excitement. Even when time moved on, and Docherty left, there was always such optimism among the fans."

In the late 1960s, Chinn, who was just 10, wrote a letter of support to a group of shareholders plotting the first great Villa revolution. He still has their reply in his study. In 1968, those supporters successfully helped to unseat the board of directors ("Villa's old guard") after a dramatic public meeting at Digbeth Civic Hall. Against all odds they shook off the cobwebs of years of decay. Ironically, it was a move that first helped to install Doug Ellis in the chairman's office. According to Chinn, history could be about to repeat itself. He is sickened and appalled by Villa's current decline. Defeat against Birmingham City was the final straw. He feels he can stay silent no longer.

"It's time for a second revolution," he said. "Unless there's a radical change at the club I don't think I'll ever see Villa as one of football's greats again. The club is in terminal decline and it breaks my heart. We've been a failure on the pitch for 20 years. Off the field we lack verve, purpose and imagination. the club has stopped reaching out to its fans. We don't belong any more, we're just customers now. It's difficult to feel passion at a club where the fans have been excluded and that's what makes the atmosphere inside the ground so subdued.

"But things will change. The time has come for true supporters to come together and stand up for what they believe. The club needs a radical overhaul. If there's to be a revolution then I will stand up and support it.

"If Doug Ellis has the interests of the club at heart he should not let the good work he has done be washed away by increasing disillusionment. He must accept responsibility for the unrest and think seriously. If he doesn't have the money or the inclination to move the club forward then he should allow people with cash, commitment and imagination to come foward and help push Villa back into a position of prominence in English football. I know those people are around. But they won't show their hands until they can sense a massive change."

Chinn certainly has the ability to mobilise support. An historian "from the day I learnt to speak", he grew to love his city and its people while sitting behind the counter of his father's bookmaker's shop. He would listen intently as punters told their stories of "old Brum" He was awarded his doctorate in 1986 and was appointed MBE two years ago. This year he became a professor. As a skilful orator, he has become a regular radio presenter in the Midlands. As an author, his twentieth book, *Birmingham Irish: Making Our Mark*, was launched last night.

His greatest moment, however, came in the spring of 2000 when 80,000 people supported a march he organised to save the Rover car factory at Longbridge from closure. He was instrumental in keeping the plant open when, from the outset, his personal crusade seemed doomed to failure.

"On the day I die, I'll see those 80,000 ordinary folks and remember how proud I was to march with them," he said, foaming with emotion. "We had such passion and fervour - they are the two most important words in my vocabulary.

Without passion humans might as well be made out of clay. We also had hope, even though we knew it was an impossible fight.

"Hope is also what keeps football fans going," he said. "Talking to you and reliving past times has made me realise why I'm a Villa fan. We all have dreams, mine is to watch Villa win the FA Cup before I die. I desperately want to see my club become a dominant force again and Villa Park become a place of excellence. But I'm beginning to despair. And I'm not alone. All around I see hope fading.

"And, you ask any football fan. A life without hope is a life not worth living."

As a direct result of this article, supporters and shareholders united under the banner "Villa Fans Combined" (VFC) to ensure a "root-and-branch" change in the way their club was being "owned and run". VFC issued an open letter to supporters, and published a blueprint for the club's future.

"It is a call to arms for fans who, in recent seasons, have been crying out for a voice," a spokesman said. "With such uncertainty running throughout the club this season, VFC says only a change at board level can arrest the cycle of stagnation and slump which has become the Aston Villa story."

The Villa revolution 2003, thanks to "Brum's the Word", was finally underway.

We'll be there, at the end of the road

Saturday, March 29, 2003.

A SMALL, GINGER-HAIRED boy clings to his father's hand. "Dad," he says fishing frantically inside his coat pocket, "you've forgotten to kiss my programme."

His father is wearing a yellow and green striped shirt, the away colours of West Bromwich Albion. On the back it reads "Proud 2 be a Baggie". Dutifully, he pecks the front page of his son's Birmingham City match-day magazine. He returns it with a sigh. "I've kissed your programme before every game and we've only won five times this season," he said. "I'm not sure it works."

His pessimistic mood is reflected on the faces of hundreds more in the visitors' enclosure at St Andrew's. There's an air of gentle resignation among those here to witness Albion's "last stand" against their local rivals. They're the same bunch of hardy faithfuls who gathered full of hope and gushing with nervous excitement for the opening game at Old Trafford seven months ago. Then, the magical adventure was just beginning. Now, a gruelling Premiership campaign has taken its toll. These fans are weary, almost punch-drunk. "No money spent during the transfer window. It's a joke. We never really gave ourselves a chance," one man said, devouring a meat pie underneath the romantically named Railway End. "Megson's lost the plot," another added. "Not one penalty all season? The Premier League is bent," a third scoffed. Some remain blindly optimistic. "You never know. Our season might start here," one lady who everybody knows as Auntie Val shrieked.

This is the friendly second-city derby, a world apart from the Aston Villa - Birmingham game just 19 days ago. There's no venom in the air. The atmosphere on the way to the ground is almost like that of a church bazaar. Fans shake hands and walk together up the Coventry Road - the main drag that leads from the city centre to St Andrew's. The common theme is Premiership survival. "I hope you stay up," appears to be the simple, heartfelt message on everyone's lips. There's no hint of intimidation. Far removed from the frightening scenes before, during and after the two games between Blues and Villa.

Nobody is sure why, but there's a mutual respect between these two sets of supporters. That's the way it's always been - and that's the way it probably always will be. Most Albion fans despise Wolverhampton Wanderers. Closer to the city centre, you are either a Bluenose or a Villain and never the twain shall meet. But when the Baggies play Blues, nobody really dislikes anybody. It's one of football's great peculiarities.

The mood spreads to the players, too. Paul Durkin, the referee, is about to embark on the quietest afternoon of his season. Not once did he contemplate a caution, let alone a red card. The genial atmosphere was epitomised when Clinton Morrison, the Birmingham striker, fell to the ground after a clattering challenge from Neil Clement. The Albion defender insisted play be halted even though his side were on the attack.

By contrast Dion Dublin and Joey Gudjonsson were given their marching orders at Villa Park as the game against Birmingham on March 3 degenerated into a shameful spectacle. Dublin felt the need to apologise the following day for head-butting Birmingham midfielder Robbie Savage. The two players have allegedly received death threats from fans since the incident.

Both matches between Villa and Blues were marred by constant, threatening pitch invasions. The only intrusion onto the playing surface during the Albion game came when the Birmingham bench piled onto the field as one, twirling their tracksuit tops, after Geoff Horsfield's scrappy winner four minutes into injury time. For Blues, it was a valuable three points. They will finish the season unbeaten in all their local derby games. With Villa unable to halt their appalling slide, I would bet good money on Steve Bruce's team ending their first term back in the top flight for 16 years, as the highest placed club in the West Midlands. Football in the area really has reached its "tipping point".

For Albion, the goal was a bitter pill to swallow, a crushing final blow that virtually condemned them to Nationwide League first division football next season. The harsh reality of relegation had sunk in at last and, on the final whistle, there followed scenes usually reserved for the last day of the season. To quote the famous old Birmingham City anthem, Albion had reached the end of the road - and everyone knew it.

One young man slumped into his seat holding his head in his hands, it was too much for him to take in. He wasn't alone. Another made no attempt to restrain the tears while his wife gazed blankly into the distance, gripping her steel walking frame. On an afternoon when football was far from the most important event in an uncertain world, these fans were inconsolable. Baggies manager Gary Megson described the result as "disastrous".

Even now, an announcement wishing West Bromwich Albion "all the best for the rest of the season" was greeted by a warm and genuine round of applause from the Birmingham fans closest to the away end in the Spion Kop - the same fans that had snarled at, and provoked, travelling Aston Villa supporters a few months earlier.

BRUM'S THE WORD

In response, the Albion followers drummed up a last and defiant chorus of *The Lord is My Shepherd*. It's become their theme tune and it was a fitting end to proceedings.

This was Albion's wake.

The final nail had been hammered into their Premiership coffin in the cruellest fashion. Although for many, the injury time goal fittingly summed up what has been a luckless first season in the Premiership. Albion's shattered players left the field in total disillusionment

The ginger-haired boy looked solemnly at his father. "Do you think we'll be back, Dad?" he asked, still clutching his programme.

His Dad heard the question. His stare, however, was fixed on the field. He was determined to applaud each and every one of "his boys" off the park. Finally, he glanced down at his feet. Turning once more to his son, he shook his head in disbelief. "Yes, of course we will," he said. "Of course we will."

Striker whose goal is to erase the memories of war

Saturday, April 5, 2003.

JASPER CARROTT'S showbusiness career began there. Zat Knight, the Fulham defender, had his dreams of stardom dented there. Now the leafy home of Colinthains Football Club on the corner of Lugtrout Lane in Solihull is again about to be thrust into the limelight - thanks to the splendidly named Elvis Music.

Elvis (yes, that is his real name) has scored 16 goals for Colinthians in the Birmingham AFA premier division this season, even though his team are struggling at the foot of the table. But this isn't a story about his quirky name or his football prowess. Elvis, a Bosnian refugee, has a harrowing human tale to tell. As a young lad growing up in the town of Prijedor, he witnessed, first hand, the horrors of war and ethnic cleansing that swept through his homeland.

His memories are disturbing. "I can talk to you all day, but a thousand words could never describe the terror we went through," he said. "People watch pictures of the Gulf War every night on television - I do it myself - but they still can't begin to understand." He gazed straight ahead. "War is one terrible thing. You have to go through it to appreciate the true horror."

His life changed dramatically one spring day in 1992. Normality had disappeared overnight. His school surrounded by Serb tanks and soldiers gathered menacingly in makeshift bunkers. Classes, that day, were filled with an eerie silence. Sitting in the front room of his Moseley home, with his mother, Hava, at his side, Elvis slowly recounted the early days of Bosnia's "circle of hell" when "the streets were filled with fire, death and destruction."

"I remember when Serb soldiers came to my house," he said. "They told us to put white flags out, then they stole what they needed and ordered us to walk to the end of the street. As I looked back, I saw them burn our home to the ground. In one day, my mother lost everything she had ever worked for. But we had no choice. I was watching innocent people being killed. My uncle was taken to the back of the house, shot dead and thrown into a hole. It was his grave.

"We were left with absolutely nothing. What wasn't taken was burnt."

Elvis, whose father died when he was six months old, was sent with his mother and two sisters to a concentration camp in Travnik, then moved on again to Croatia.

"When we were in Croatia, we suffered the worst day of all," he said. "We were herded into an air-raid shelter. I sat with my back to the wall next to my mother. The noise was frightening. There was heavy bombing all around and I felt sure I was going to die - for a young boy it's a terrible thought. The ground was shaking and you could hear buildings crumbling and glass shattering. Some people chose to stay with their homes - they didn't want to leave, because it was all they had. When we came out the scenes were awful. Dead people in the street. Arms and legs everywhere. I'll never forget it."

Even before the war, times were hard for Elvis, who got his name because his mother was a fan of the "King of Rock'n'Roll" (Music is a common surname in Bosnia). Bringing up the family alone, Hava was struggling to make ends meet, working long hours in a toilet roll factory. Football could have been the family's route out of the poverty trap. As a six-year-old, Elvis caught the bug, kicking a ball for up to ten hours a day around the shabby streets of his humble hometown. When he was just 9, he was snapped up by FK Rudar Ugljevik, a Bosnia-Herzegovina Premier League side. Many other clubs were keen to sign him. "But the war robbed me of the chance to play professionally," he said. "It robbed me of everything."

Even so, Elvis considers himself lucky. Through the Red Cross, his family were able to flee Croatia and move to Birmingham. "We had nothing, knew nobody and couldn't speak a word of English," he said. But they soon settled down - and football again became his salvation.

Colinthians became his new team. They run four sides from a humble base, although their clubhouse is home to the legendary Boggery Folk Club, where Jasper Carrott took his first tentative steps to stardom in the 1960s. Zat Knight began his football career there but never made the first team. He later moved to Rushall Olympic and eventually to Craven Cottage.

This season has been a tough one for The Cols. Despite the goal scoring exploits of Elvis, they have won only one game. But the Bosnian striker is unperturbed. "I play for the love of the game now," he said. "In a way, football has kept me going. It has been my release."

Elvis, now 24 and working as a security guard for a local company, is content with his new life - but his old one is never far away. Nightly images of the war in Iraq bring his own vivid memories flooding back. "It's the innocent civilians I feel for. They are trapped. They won't know what to believe or who to trust - we didn't. They will just be praying to be left alone, to continue their lives in peace."

At least normality has been restored in Bosnia. Elvis has had the plot of land where his home once stood returned to him. He is determined to raise enough money to build a house so his mother can return. But he has no plans to go back himself. He has a job, his friends - and a tough game for

Colinthians against Old Wulfrunians, who are top of the table, this afternoon.

"The people of Bosnia have finally come back together," he said. "They are friends again. They drink together. But whenever they talk about the war, they always reach the same conclusion: everybody lost."

Evergreen Brown still bowling along nicely

Saturday, April 12, 2003.

NESTLING IN THE SHADOW of The Hawthorns, within a Russell Hoult goalkick of West Bromwich Albion's centre circle, there lies a more humble sports arena. Half a dozen park benches are enough to comfortably house the spectators. The floodlight pylons hardly dominate the Black Country skyline, dwarfed by their towering and precisely angled bright white counterparts across the road.

Behind a rickety garden gate, all is revealed. Scrawled on a blackboard are the words "keep off the grass". A small sign welcomes visitors to The Throstles Bowling Club. It has been here for 55 years. This afternoon, almost 30,000 people will walk past it on their way to watch Albion play Everton. Few will take any notice. Most won't even realise it's there.

But this partially hidden, beautifully manicured green has, in its own way, witnessed just as much drama as its famous big brother on the other side of Halfords Lane. On Wednesday evening, the curtain opens on a new season for one of the club's newly promoted teams. It is going to be a big night. Not least for Alistair Brown, the former Albion striker, who will be playing, as usual, for the home side as they embark on their new bowls campaign. Ally, as he is affectionately known, has sampled life on both sides of the road.

An Albion stalwart for 11 years, he scored 85 goals in 359 appearances. He was the top goal scorer in Ron Atkinson's 1978 team that finished third in the old first division and reached the quarter-finals of the Uefa Cup before being knocked out by Red Star Belgrade on a heart-stopping Hawthorns evening. Now, at 52, he has become a keen crown green bowler. He has swapped the goals and the glory for the toucher, the bobby and the thumb bias. Once, he played for a title-chasing Baggies side at Old Trafford and Anfield. Now he "plays the knob" in the Oldbury League third division (It's a sporting term for using the crown of the green to good advantage).

Brown, who still cuts a lean sporting figure - "I'm only a stone heavier than my football weight," - took up his new sport eight years ago when he became full-time steward of the Throstle Club, the Albion fans' official headquarters and pre-match drinking den, which looks out onto the green.

"It's a great game," he said, deep in concentration. He carefully eyes up his wood and caresses it before elegantly launching it over the "Throstle hump" towards a static jack some 20 yards away. It's just before 10am on a Monday morning but he is getting in some practice for Wednesday's season-opener against Coombswood, from Halesowen. "It's intriguing. You have to read the lie of the land, negotiate the hollows and the humps. It's just like hitting the perfect golf putt," he added sending another wood jack-bound.

"It's relaxing, but I'm very competitive when I play," Brown said. He's still every inch the marksman and, although now content to show off his skills in front of around two dozen eager onlookers, he's just as hungry for victory. "I want to win every time I bowl. There's no point in playing if you don't want to succeed. I was the same as a footballer - but, these days, I think I'm a little more gracious in defeat.

"People think crown green bowls is an old man's sport. But that's a myth," he said. "When I go home to Scotland I see greens that are full of youngsters. They start young and that's why the country is so well represented at the big tournaments."

Brown was born in Musselburgh. His father worked in a local paper mill, but his uncle, Willie Bauld, was crowned "King of Tynecastle" in the 1950s for his goal scoring exploits with Heart of Midlothian. Ally was spotted by a Leicester City scout while playing for Musselburgh Grammar in the Scottish Schools Cup final. He scored from a free kick - and so began his professional career. "I've been here since 1966, a bad year for Scottish football," he said. "Apart from the accent, I'm almost completely English now."

Don Howe signed him for Albion for the peculiar sum of £61,111 in 1972.

"Ron Saunders wanted me to join Norwich City but when I heard Albion were interested I didn't have to think twice," Brown, who soon became a Hawthorns favourite, said. He scored on his first two senior outings for the club, was chauffeur to Willie Johnston, the club's hot-headed Scotland international winger ("I remember we had a terrible bust up on the training field one day - but I still drove him home."), and was room-mate of Brendon Batson, the defender who is now Albion managing director - and, therefore, Ally's boss.

Brown was also part of the squad that was given an "intriguing and unexpected" team talk by Edward Heath, the former Prime Minister, before their historical trip to China in the summer of 1978. "We were the first Western side to visit the country and he turned up in the dressing-room to emphasis how important the tour was. He was keen for us to be on our best behaviour. He told us we were serving the whole of the Western world - and not just our country."

Today, as usual, Brown will be serving pre-match pints to the fans that once worshipped him from the terraces. If results go badly, he may have to deal with hundreds of disconsolate Baggies supporters, trudging their way slowly back over the road to drown their sorrows with relegation from the Barclaycard Premiership finally confirmed.

BRUM'S THE WORD

After soaking up the moans, groans and spilt beer, he'll then set his sights on Wednesday night. The Throstles Bowling Club has 45 members and runs teams in four different summer leagues. Brown's side was one of two that won promotion last term. Hope springs eternal for more glory this time around.

On one side of the road, it seems, they can wait for the season to start - on the other they can't wait for it to finish.

* Matthew Humphries, via email from Darlaston, writes: "I was intrigued by your column on Ally Brown - he was one of my Albion heroes, although my father insisted on calling him "twinkle toes", much to my annoyance. It's fascinating that Edward Heath called the team together for a pre-tour briefing before the club's historical trip to China. If my memory serves me correctly, one of the Baggies players, on arriving at the Great Wall, was heard to say, 'I've bent free-kicks around better walls than that.' So much for representing the whole of the civilised Western world!"

* West Bromwich Albion's inevitable relegation to the Nationwide League, first division, was finally confirmed on Saturday, April 19. The Baggies beat Sunderland 2-1 at the Stadium of Light. But the three points were not enough because of Bolton's victory over West Ham. Gary Megson, the Albion manager, said after the match: "It's been a strange afternoon - to win a game away from home and then find out we've been relegated in doing so."

Ross finds ways to turn airwaves blue

Saturday, April 19, 2003.

A TINY, YET INTRICATE, electric guitar sits on the shelf next to a replica of the World Cup.

Nearby, a tattered season ticket book containing passes for Aston Villa's official car park lies beside a box of Birmingham City after-dinner chocolates. The office walls are randomly scattered with signed gold and silver discs. This is the world of Tom Ross. "Rossy". A one hundred per cent radio man - and fiercely proud of it.

Soon, he will take a brisk walk from desk to microphone to host Britain's longest running football phone-in, a show invented by Tony Butler, a broadcasting legend far beyond the boundaries of Birmingham, more than 30 years ago. Ross is a disciple of his predecessor, but he does things very differently. He will sit with his feet up, virtually sprawled out across an area no bigger than the famous soundproof booth, once used by contestants on the 1970s quiz show, *Mr and Mrs*. It's his way of talking to the fans. "I try and create a pub atmosphere," he said, eager to demonstrate his broadcasting stance.

"This is not just a job," he insisted, carefully drinking in his surroundings - the mystical world of the radio studio. "It's my life. I'm the luckiest man in the world." He's quick to add a note of caution, though. "But I'll be a working class Brummie until the day I die."

Ross is known as one of the hardest grafters in the radio industry. His day starts at 6am when he hosts the breakfast show from the headquarters of BRMB/Capital Gold in Birmingham's fashionable Brindleyplace. After that, as the station's Head of Sport, he begins a routine whistlestop tour of the training grounds on his patch. He is greeted as a friend by players and managers alike. Often, he will then travel to commentate on a match (he calls every commentary game "an event"). If it's a long trip, he will arrive back in the city at around 2am to start all over again, after less than four hours sleep. On top of that, he will somehow squeeze in two hours at the gym.

The boy from "two back of 437, New John Street West - Aston" has done good. So good that he's been nominated for a Sony Award - the Oscars of the radio business. The ceremony takes place in London next month.

"Sometimes I have to pinch myself," Ross said. "There were six kids in our house and we had nothing. Mum was a cleaner and barmaid at the Britannia pub. Dad was amazing. He could get four hundred slices from a Swiss roll. You could see through each slice."

As an eight-year-old boy, Ross fell hopelessly in love with Birmingham City after his Scottish father, also Tom, who is now 90-years-old, began walking to St Andrew's to watch his fellow countryman Alex Govan, in action. Govan was the man who first sang the Blues anthem *Keep Right on to the End of the Road* on the way to Birmingham's 1956 FA Cup quarter-final against Arsenal. The song spread quickly among the players - and then to the fans.

"We reached the FA Cup final that year," Ross said, with a twinkle in his eye. "I remember thinking - 'this is the team for me, sixth in division one and a visit to Wembley'. How they lead me on! But football slowly seeped into my blood. I used to stand on the Kop with my school pal, Connie Walsh - and I always took my boots, just in case. That's the kind of kid I was - a head full of dreams and a heart full of hope."

Ross dreamt of a career in professional football. He played left back for Hinckley Athletic in the Southern League. "We got ten bob a week and our own shirts - having the kit was worth more than the money. And I never worried how quick the wingers were, as long as they could hurdle. I'd go in hard on anybody, always giving everything to win a game of football for my lads. But I would never cheat."

That sums up Tom Ross. "I'm a perfectionist. A one hundred per cent man. I worry about every radio show I present," he said. "My Dad once told me: 'Never be ashamed to pick up your wages'. Since then I've always worked my socks off. If they put the words, 'hard-working, loyal and honest on my tombstone' - I'll be happy."

Ross knew his dreams of becoming a professional footballer were doomed when the Hinckley manager left him stranded in Castle Bromwich one weekend. "He used to give me a lift to every game - but one afternoon he didn't turn up. He rang me the following week to say that because I was his most enthusiastic player, he hadn't got the heart to tell me I wasn't good enough. Good job he phoned - I'd still be waiting now."

Instead, Ross set out on the media path, although he is still player-manager of Birmingham City Old Stars. His first match as a radio reporter was a Blues friendly against Ajax. He has hosted the Friday night phone-in for almost 20 years.

One of Ross's most memorable moments came during Birmingham's Leyland Daf Cup final against Tranmere Rovers in 1991. "I became the first reporter to commentate from the bench at Wembley," he said. "Lou Macari, the Birmingham manager, put me down on the teamsheet as second physio. We smuggled the microphone and headphones past officials in a bucket."

Now, despite his unashamed Blues bent, he's largely accepted by fans of the other Midlands clubs, but he's always a target for "friendly fire". His golden oldie breakfast show feeds the other great passion in his life. "Music and football - they are the star players in the theatre of your mind," he said. "People remember their first record and the first game they went to. I'm passionate about both - I'm a Bruce Springsteen fanatic, I never miss a gig."

The curtain is about to rise on another performance. Ross pauses. His "wonderful city" is waiting to debate the sporting issues of the day. "I'm not that important, you know," he said. "This beautiful invention called football is only about the players and the fans - the day we forget that is the day the game dies."

* Tom Ross received a silver Sony award at the 2003 ceremony, which took place at London's Grosvenor House Hotel on Thursday, May 8. The gold award went to a BBC 5 Live programme entitled: 'Football Finance: The Bankrupt Game'.

Rogers relishing the drama that is City

Saturday, April 26, 2003.

THURSDAY, APRIL 17, 2003…A day that will be catalogued in the history of Birmingham forever. A group of firefighters hose down the charred remains of one of the city's most famous landmarks - Raymond Mason's *Forward* sculpture. One takes a hefty swipe at the base of the statue with a lump hammer. On a nearby patio overlooking Centenary Square, Stuart Rogers, executive director of the Birmingham Repertory Theatre, shakes his head in disbelief. "I hope this isn't an omen for next season," he said.

It's the sort of response that could only come from a Birmingham City fan, a breed noted for their pessimism.

Rogers carefully watches the drama unfold. The Rep looks out onto the square where the statue once proudly stood. Now it has been destroyed before his eyes.

Behind him, in large blue letters, the theatre proudly advertises the return of Matthew Kelly in *Of Mice and Men*, the John Steinbeck classic. Rogers has helped to drag the Birmingham Rep out of the doldrums. In just 18 months, he and Jonathan Church, the artistic director, have turned its fortunes around. But he wouldn't be here at all if he hadn't been lured by the irresistible call of St Andrew's.

The boy from Alum Rock was destined to become a Bluenose. "Coming from that side of the city, if you were remotely interested in football, you wouldn't dream of supporting anyone else. I didn't realise I had a choice," he said.

St Andrew's was a ten-minute bus ride from the Rogers family home and his uncle Dennis worked as a turnstile operator, which meant free entry into the main stand. It was the dream scenario.

"My first game was in 1964, under floodlights against Bristol City. I still recall the sharpness and intensity of the colours, made even more extraordinary and vivid under the bright lights. The blue and white of Birmingham, the green of the pitch, and the red shirts of the visiting team. It was an unbelievable experience for a ten year old. I also remember that Colin Green, the Blues fullback, broke his leg during the game. The whole ground went silent - you could almost hear the crunch. Unforgettable."

His first Blues idol was Geoff Vowden - "A big old-fashioned centre forward with chiselled, action hero looks," he said. "But the key moment was when Trevor Francis arrived. That's when I realised I had become wedded to the club."

Francis, and the game of football, had romanced him, but off the field Rogers fell under the spell of the theatre when a teacher at King Edward's School began an out-of-hours drama club. "Because we were at a boy's school, it was the only way of meeting girls - so I signed up," he explained.

When he got a part-time job at the city's Alexandra Theatre, his life changed forever. "I became Les Dawson's dresser during the pantomime season. It was the best job I've had in my life. We sat for hours in his room. Les in his underpants reading poetry to me while we drank gin from his minibar. He told me how, as a teenager, he ran away to Paris to become a poet - his work was very good and he was a really lovely man.

"He spent the whole eight weeks telling me to get a proper career - I came away desperate to work in the theatre."

Rogers became theatre programmer for the innovative Birmingham Arts Lab in Newtown, when he was just 18. Eventually he left his native city and, after many years working at theatres across the country, was made head of Teatro Kismet, a leading Italian company, based in Bari. In January 2002 he "came home", swapping the beaches of southern Italy for a seat in the main stand at St Andrew's. He didn't have to think twice.

"The first thing I did was renew my season ticket," he said. "I had always kept my passion for Blues alive - I flew home to watch them in the Worthington Cup final. I love being a fan. It's part of my roots and it's become more important as I've grown older - it's a vital link to my early life."

Rogers thrives on the emotional roller coaster ride that goes with the territory of being a Blues fan. "More than anything, I adore the relegation and promotion battles," he said. "My partner, Judy, is a Tottenham fan. I can't understand it. She spends most of her life watching meaningless mid-table matches. At Blues we're always on a knife-edge, but the fans have also inherited a sense of fatality. If you always look on the dark side of life, occasionally you'll be pleasantly surprised."

Rogers and Church have been stunned at the way the Rep has been transformed since they took charge. "It's phenomenal," Rogers said, "but it's not a miracle - just common sense. Being part of a theatre management team is similar to being in football - it has the same rhythm about it. We have given ourselves five years to make this place the best repertory theatre in Britain.

"It's about providing shows that people want to come and see. Theatre folk say it's difficult to have high quality productions that are also popular. We've proved them wrong with *Of Mice and Men* - in a sense we've achieved the double. That's why the 'house full' signs are out and the place is buzzing again."

For Matthew Kelly, the play marks a return to The Rep for the first time since January when he was arrested after allegations of sexual abuse against boys, during the theatre's

Christmas production of *Peter Pan*, where he played Captain Hook.

Kelly's name was cleared, but it's a period that Rogers will always remember. "It was one thing we certainly didn't expect - but Matthew was so strong and centred. He got us through it. He was loved by everybody he worked with and didn't want to run away - why should he? He was innocent. Instead he brought the company together and the way he behaved has helped to shift the nation's opinion about trial by tabloids.

"I remember waiting nervously with him when he returned to the production after his arrest," Rogers said. "We stood shoulder to shoulder in the wings before his first entrance. Although Jonathan Church and I were determined to defend him to the hilt, neither of us knew how the people of Birmingham would react. He received a spontaneous standing ovation. The audience that night spoke for the nation. I had this feeling of wonderful relief - not too dissimilar to watching Blues avoid relegation."

* *Two wins over the Easter weekend gave Birmingham City their Barclaycard Premiership lifeline. Blues beat Charlton Athletic 2-0 at The Valley before a 3-2 victory against FA Cup finalists Southampton in front of their home fans. Steve Bruce's side ended the season with a flurry. A 3-0 victory over Middlesbrough on April 26, the club's seventh win in their last nine matches, was described by many supporters as the best Birmingham league performance for many years. The three points guaranteed Premiership survival.*

* *"It's been the toughest season of my career, but also the most satisfying," Bruce said after the Middlesbrough match. "Keeping the club in the Premiership has been the biggest achievement of my entire career."*

BRUM'S THE WORD

* Dear Malcolm,

A brief note to thank you for your splendid article in The Times. It made me smile and my partner, Judy, is very impressed that you have as good a knowledge of what I'm like after our one-hour chat, as she has managed to grasp after ten years living with me.

Best wishes, Stuart Rogers
(Executive Director, Birmingham Repertory Theatre).

Albion fans dressed for (lack of) success

Saturday, May 3, 2003.

PYJAMAS AT PORTMAN ROAD - that's how it all began in the mid-1970s.

By the turn of the decade, fashions had changed. Pyjamas were out. Beachwear became the new trend for a trip to Boothferry Park. The 1990s witnessed lounge suits at Loftus Road and togas at Bristol Rovers. Now, dedicated followers of football fashion are about to turn their attentions to Ewood Park - and a planned invasion of referees. Billed as the *Men in Black* (burn), it's West Bromwich Albion's traditional end-of-season fancy dress knees-up.

Themed pageants on the last away day of the season have become a way of life for Baggies fans. They've been an annual event for almost 30 years.

This afternoon, "as a mark of respect" to Premiership officials who have awarded relegated Albion just one penalty all season, the fans will become referees for the day. Throughout the Black Country, supporters have been begging, borrowing and sometimes stealing their outfits in preparation for what they are labelling "An end-of-term celebration".

Many of the costumes are home made. Others have been specially commissioned. Oldbury-based ACE Embroidery has been inundated with requests for tailor-made shirts. In less than two weeks they have turned out more than a thousand. "It's nothing new for us," Ron Smart, a Baggies season ticket-holder who runs the company with wife

BRUM'S THE WORD

Marylyn, said. "We're often called upon for end of season outfits. I'll do anything for these fans - I've even made Albion knickers. This season, I've had to stock up on as much black material as possible."

It is estimated that there will be around 4,500 referees at the game. (4,504 if you include the official officials). Many will have the full black strip with notebook and pencil. Some will take a linesman's flag for effect - nearly all will be flashing a red or yellow card. A Dudley-based firm, Willow Print, has provided 2,000 for Baggies Travel Club members.

Others have made their own digital substitute boards showing the number 15 in protest at the stubborn reluctance of Gary Megson, the manager, to include Bob Taylor, a Hawthorns hero, in his squad this season. In his testimonial year, most fans feel that Taylor (who wears the number 15 shirt) should at least be considered for the last two meaningless matches. Some are campaigning for him to be handed the captain's armband.

But the main emphasis is on light relief - desperately needed after Albion's 6-0 thrashing by Liverpool at The Hawthorns last weekend. One fan will wear a toilet seat around his head. He will be going as Urinal Rennie. Another will place a selection of salad leaves in his top pocket. "I'm David C-Elleray" he told me as organisers put the finishing touches to the carnival at a planning meeting in West Bromwich this week. A third proudly waved a retractable washing line prop in front of my face. He will be Graham Pole.

"That's nothing," Dave "The Commander" Holloway, the Baggies Travel Club organiser, who will be in charge of 20 coaches leaving the Hawthorns at 10.30am this morning, said. "The president of the supporters' club is painting his face green. He's Paul Gurkin. The only thing we won't tolerate is whistles," the Commander added. "That could lead to carnage. We don't want the game to degenerate into a farce."

BRUM'S THE WORD

Even referees of the past will be honoured. One supporter is taking his child's mini-keyboard. He has styled himself as Raymond Tinkler, the referee who awarded the infamous Jeff Astle goal that robbed Leeds United of the first division title in 1971. "We couldn't give a monkey's that we've just suffered our worst home defeat ever," Commander Holloway said. "In fact, the game against Liverpool underlined our point. Television cameras showed that Jason Roberts's second-half effort crossed the line. Even though we were 6-0 down, the referee refused to give us the benefit of the doubt. That's life as an unfashionable Premiership club."

The theatrical bent of many Albion fans and their infatuation with fancy dress after a long season of terrace torment, has been studied by husband-and-wife duo Simon and Glynis Wright - co-editors of the club's *Grorty Dick* fanzine.

"Nothing like this happens anywhere else in the country - certainly not on the scale we do it," Glynis said. "The trend began in the 1970s when, for some unknown reason, fans started to wear pyjamas when the club visited Ipswich Town. Beachwear was introduced at Hull City in 1989. One fan even smuggled a surfboard into the ground. In 2000, Albion supporters were judged to be the scruffiest in football - so the end-of-season theme at Queen's Park Rangers was lounge suits, dinner jackets and cocktail dresses. One woman went the whole hog and wore a tiara."

One of the saddest end-of-term fancy dress balls came against Bristol Rovers at Twerton Park in 1991. A visit to the Roman city of Bath prompted the fans to kit themselves out in togas. But a 1-1 draw meant the team, managed by Bobby Gould, was relegated for the first time to the old third division.

"Fortunately we made amends when we played Shrewsbury Town the following year," Glynis said. "Nearly two thousand Albion fans dressed up as undertakers to celebrate Gould's imminent departure. A coffin baring his name was ceremonially paraded through the streets of the town."

At Blackburn the mood will be less sombre. It will be a last opportunity for Baggie die-hards to show football's ruling classes how to have a good time in the face of adversity. After all, next season it could be choo-choos at Crewe or merry millers at Millmoor. "As long as it's not a trip to Wigan," one worried fan said. "I don't fancy dressing up as a pier."

* As well as a huge turnout of referees, one fan attended the Blackburn Rovers game dressed as a giraffe. Another went as a penguin, while a third managed to get hold of a convincing ant-eater costume. During a lull in the match, Albion fans entertained themselves by chanting, "There's only one giraffe" and "Giraffe, giraffe give us a wave".

The giraffe, who kept his three foot "head" on throughout the match, duly obliged with a hearty wave, much to the delight of his fellow Baggies supporters.

Bob Taylor, dressed as a referee, sat with the supporters having been left out of the Albion starting squad.

Bull brothers united
in rise to top

Saturday, May 10, 2003.

GEORGE BULL takes me to one side. It's "Variety Thursday" at the Tipton Sports and Social Club and the smoke-filled function room is brimming with enthusiastic punters. "Where else would you get a night like this for just £5?" George asks, patting my shoulder.

The father of Wolverhampton Wanderers legend Steve has hit the nail on the head. In the Black Country, this is entertainment of the highest quality.

Outside the humble auditorium, posters advertising "tennis for beginners" compete with blackboard notices that boast forthcoming star attractions. Go through a set of double doors, and you enter another world. On stage, two sisters are belting out a gutsy rendition of the Cher classic *Believe* while an accompanying organist valiantly attempts to keep up with the tempo. They are one of 12 turns on tonight's bill, which was "kicked off", in the words of the host, by a pair of young ladies in sequined black leotards and silver top hats dancing to the Liza Minelli smash hit *Cabaret*.

Joan Bull, Steve's mother and a West Bromwich Albion supporter since she was 8, sits at a small table in the corner of the room. She has been taking the entrance money. Joan is poised for a long night. It's her job to "run the artists back home" after their stint in the spotlight. At the end of the evening she'll haul the hefty speakers, microphones and mixing desk into the back of her Peugeot. "I'm the ticket inspector and roadie," she said, proudly. "It's alright though, I've got a decent car. Steven bought it for me as a Christmas box two years ago."

Next on stage is 12-year-old Natasha Bennett. "She was Karen Carpenter on *Stars in Your Eyes Kids*," George told me, as she took her place in front of the off-red velvet curtains. An air of expectancy falls on a room packed to capacity with heavily made-up ladies in posh frocks and the occasional stocky gent who would rather be at home with his ferrets. Sadly, before Natasha has chance to launch into her number, the compere interrupts. "If anybody would like to take part in *Play Your Cards Right* next door, can they please see Geoff at the bar," he said.

The star attraction of the night is Alan Bull, Steve's brother and youngest son of George and Joan. He's also the organiser of "Variety Thursday" - and a worried man. "It's running late. We won't finish till midnight," he said, in his broad Black Country accent. Alan's a born worrier, but when he performs he becomes the consummate entertainer. Tonight his brother and four sisters Linda, Kim, Jane and Lillian will provide moral support alongside mum and dad. This is very much a family affair. Bull gatherings always are.

And it's been a monumental week for them all. Steve, Wolves' record goal scorer, has been informed that a stand at Molineux is to be named in his honour. Meanwhile, Alan has released his first record *Hey Jonesy* in celebration at the club reaching the promotion play-offs. The lyrics are "Hey, hey Jonesy - ohh ahh - we wanna go-ooo to the Premier League", sang to the tune of the 1962 Bruce Channel hit *Hey! Baby*.

The two boys have been signing the CDs all week in preparation for this afternoon's first play-off game against Reading - and it's been going down a storm. Almost 1,000 willing customers queued at the Merry Hill Centre last weekend. "I didn't have to wait this long for Father

Christmas," one excited elderly lady dressed in Wolves top and floral skirt, said.

When they pose for the camera, the Bull brothers are united by the ability to woo a crowd. They are both born entertainers - but in very different worlds.

Alan, at 29 the baby of the family, admits to knowing nothing about football. "I don't understand it in the slightest," he confessed. "And I'm absolutely rubbish at playing. My legs are too skinny. I used to love going to watch Steve in action for Wolves, but I hadn't really got a clue what was going on. I don't know the foggiest thing about the offside rule. All I know is that you cheer when your team scores a goal.

"As youngsters, while Steve was playing football, I was listening to Five Star records on the hi-fi with my sisters. I didn't know what Old Trafford was. But it works both ways - Steve can't sing."

Steve is quick to butt in. "We're totally different in looks, build, interests - everything. Obviously I'm the handsome one, but Alan has got talent. As a singer, he can certainly hold his own."

Singing is not only Alan's passion - it helped save his life. "Three years ago I woke up with pains in my chest," he said. "The next thing I knew I was in hospital with a collapsed lung. The doctors told me I had six months to live. When I came out of hospital I took up singing to pass the time and it seemed to ease my condition. Since then, I've never looked back. Within a month I'd had my first lesson and suddenly I was on the club circuit.

"My ultimate ambition is to cut a record and make the charts. I'd love to work with Pete Waterman, although as yet, he hasn't called me."

The favourable reaction to his new Wolves record has fuelled Alan's craving to become a recording artist, but he knows it's going to be a long, hard slog. Meanwhile, at the

BRUM'S THE WORD

Tipton Sports and Social Club it's nearly midnight and some of the thrill-seekers have started to drift away. George Bull takes to the dance floor as a lofty Tina Turner look-alike from Bilston struggles with her version of *Simply the Best*. She dedicates her performance to Steve, still the region's undisputed super-hero, but deep down she knows that his brother might soon be the Bull taking fame by the horns.

Whoever's in the limelight, the rest of the family will give their full backing. "We even go to watch Alan practice," Steve said. "That's the way we are. It's part of our Tipton breeding and we'll never change. It's all about family support," he added. "I suppose we're a bit like The Waltons in that way."

Monday, March 27, 2003.

WOLVERHAMPTON WANDERERS are promoted to the Barclaycard Premiership when they demolish Sheffield United 3-0 in the first division's play-off final at the Millennium Stadium in Cardiff. First half goals by Mark Kennedy, Nathan Blake and Kenny Miller are enough to send the gold and black half of the Black Country into football ecstasy.

For Wolves owner Sir Jack Hayward, who has ploughed more than £50 million into the club since taking charge in 1990, it was the fulfilment of a Molineux dream. Hayward labelled himself the "golden tit" five years ago, indicating that he was like a mother presiding over a child that needed constant nourishment. But after the play-off victory, he promised yet more cash. He urged his team to follow in the footsteps of Birmingham City. "Whatever it costs, we have to stay there and consolidate," he said. "We have to try and do the sort of great job Birmingham have done."

Wiping away the tears with a gleaming white handkerchief, the 80-year-old, sporting his customary gold and black rosette, added in song: "Hey, hey Jonesy - ohh ahh. I wanna tha-a-a-a-ank you for the Premier League."

The Wolves adventure was just beginning.

Journey's end

Saturday, May 17, 2003.

MARGARET TURNER shovels one last batch of frozen chips into the deep fat fryer. It's been a long, hard season. "I'm glad I've got the snack bar," she said. "It's flipping hard work - but at least it takes your mind off relegation."

Margaret is a lifelong, unpaid football servant. She neither asks for, nor receives the rewards she so richly deserves. "I've done just about everything at Dudley Town," she said, moving quickly towards the tea urn, "except play for them." My season-long journey that began at the Theatre of Dreams, Old Trafford has finally come to an end in the middle of a modest housing estate in Sandwell. It's a humble backdrop - but it's still football.

A makeshift sign above the clubhouse bar reads "Welcome to The Beeches", it's the home of Dudley - a ground they share with neighbours Tividale. The "stadium" is a ramshackle affair but, when things begin to cut up rough, nerves jangle here just like they do at any venue, anywhere in the football world. It's crunch time for The Robins. They are in danger of falling out of the premier division of the Express & Star West Midland Regional League. Margaret, who is the club's long-serving secretary and general dogsbody (as well as snack bar serving wench), is starting to feel the tension.

At least Dudley have given themselves a chance of avoiding the drop by signing Mark Walters, the former Aston Villa, Glasgow Rangers and Liverpool midfielder. His presence in the starting line-up has put another 12 onto today's gate, including Glynn, who owns a Staffordshire Bull Terrier

Shop in Darlaston. He's watching intently from a handy vantage point behind the goal - just in front of Margaret's snack bar. He can almost smell the Bovril.

Walters has tasted the highs and lows of football. He was part of Aston Villa's European Super Cup winning side of 1982. He went on to help Rangers win the Premier League title, the Scottish Cup and the Skol Cup before signing for Liverpool in 1991. He hasn't moved to Dudley Town for the glory - his love of playing the game has always out-weighed the glamour it has provided for him. He's another staunch football flag waver, and proud of it.

Still in peak condition, he sits quietly under a picture of the 1982 Villa team. He looks up and points himself out, standing next to goalkeeper Nigel Spink on the back row. "They were the best days of my career," he said, wistfully. "I've spent most of my life performing in front of 40,000 people. Now I play in front of 40," he added with a grin. "But I still thrive on football. I haven't lost an ounce of passion or enthusiasm. That's the game for you. It's in your blood. Even when I was a boy, football came before everything. It still does - no matter what league you're in, it's still football."

Walters is "back home" in the Midlands after a long and fruitful football adventure that began as a teenager at Villa Park. He now spends his time coaching Villa's under-9s team at the club's "academy" - a converted indoor cricket venue behind the North Stand. He was appointed by Graham Taylor along with Tony Daley, another former Villa Park favourite.

"I always believed I was going to play football professionally. I remember crawling underneath the turnstiles to watch Villa play when I was a young boy," he said. "My mother, Ivy still lives within earshot of the ground. She can hear the roars of the Holte End."

It was Ivy who gave Walters his football break when she allowed him to skip off Sunday School to train with the Dunlop

Terriers. But, like most Villa fans, he has been disappointed by a season of under achievement. "Graham Taylor is a great manager. As a player, I learned more from him than anybody else," he said. "But we've not done ourselves justice this season. We're short of a quality and experience. We could have done with a Christophe Dugarry. Someone who can turn your season around."

Unfortunately for Villa, Dugarry is down the road at St Andrew's signing a new two-year contract. "Le Magnifique", as he's been christened by the Birmingham City fans, has helped Blues finish above Villa in the Premiership table. They have emerged from the doldrums to stake a claim for the coveted title of the Midlands' most successful club. For Villa fans like Walters, that hurts. For the city's Bluenose belt it means the world.

Steve Bruce, the Birmingham City manager who signed a new five-year contract yesterday, hails Dugarry as British football's new Eric Cantona. The greatest player the club has ever had. The St Andrew's faithful have started to worship him. He is beginning to replace Trevor Francis as their all-time hero. "He doesn't have feet, he has two magic wands," one fan said. "This is the best Birmingham team ever and Dugarry is British football's new genius."

During my personal journey over the last 40 weeks I've met many people who have made the game beautiful. The trip has taken me from the Theatre of Dreams to the Birmingham Hippodrome Theatre, via a bingo hall in Bilston, a church, a sweet factory and a crematorium. I've spoken to players past and present, supporters, celebrities, soccer pundits - and in one case a club owner's mother. Football was their uniting force. I've witnessed the relegation of West Bromwich Albion and watched Villa lose their grip as the "untouchables" of West Midlands football.

I've played a part in starting the Villa revolution. After one article, a group calling themselves Villa Fans Combined, was born - a movement that, in time, hopes to change the way the club is run forever. I was there when football in the West Midlands reached its tipping point. When the balance of power began to shift from claret and blue, to royal blue. Nobody on the patch won a thing - it's been quite a season.

It's fitting that my magical mystery tour should end in the football back-waters of Sandwell, and that I should be sat in quiet contemplation with Mark Walters. His new club, in a way, represents the true spirit of the beautiful game. These people don't take from football - they give everything. They are the real heroes. This is not just journey's end - I've also reached my goal, I've come home. I'm standing shoulder to shoulder with a group of people who have truly lost their hearts, and some might say their minds, to football.

In their final match, Dudley fought out a 3-3 draw with Heath Hayes after being three-up at half time. "I had to put my hands over my eyes for most of the second half," Margaret Turner said. The draw leaves her side third from bottom of the table. Even though the team didn't lose any of their last seven games, they will have to wait until a league meeting in June to find out their fate. That only prolongs the agony for Margaret - and fellow club stalwart Nevil Jeynes. He first got involved with The Robbins in 1966. Since then he has been secretary, treasurer and now he's chairman. He's seen the club through every peak and trough.

Mrs Turner, football heroine, begins the arduous task of clearing up the tiny snack bar for the last time this season. She's looking forward to the summer. "We always have a week in Paignton," she said smiling - for a second her mind is now focussed on the swinging palm trees of the English Riviera. "We go there every year with our dog. He's called Dudley."

Club chairman Nevil butts in. "We'll have learned our fate by then," he said, still concerned at the thought of relegation. "I don't think we'll keep players like Mark

Walters if we go down, but hopefully we'll live to fight another day.

"That's the good thing about football," he added with a half-smile. "There's always next season..."

* *Dudley Town avoided relegation because first division Bewdley's picturesque riverside ground hadn't got the necessary facilities to get them promoted. The Robbins are still playing their home matches at their temporary shared home. Margaret Turner never got to Paignton for her one-week holiday. Football business over the summer months meant she had to stay at home in Lower Gornal.*

* *Aston Villa avoided relegation by three points, finishing fifth from bottom in the Premiership with 45 points - three places below the West Midlands' most successful side, Birmingham City. Villa managed just one away league win all season.*

LE MAGNIFIQUE
A TRIBUTE TO CHRISTOPHE DUGARRY
By Paul Collins
(Chelmsley Wood taxi driver!)

He's an artist born in France, who paints pictures with his feet. With his Gallic tricks and style, he'll soon get you off your seat. Like a veteran matador, he is the master of his craft, And if it's your job to mark him, he can make you look quite daft.

In the air he hangs like a kestrel, with his feet he waves his wand. He even looks like Jesus - and he wears an Alice band! His hips they move like Elvis, he has a computer for a brain, He's surely one of the greats of our beautiful game.

BRUM'S THE WORD

He came to Brum from Bordeaux; he's like a vintage wine.
When his name is on the team sheet, you know all will be
fine. It's only air-filled leather, but he can make that baby
sing.Christophe was made for Birmingham. We've been
waiting for our king.

Dugarry's different class. His gifts were given by God.
50 odd caps and a World Cup winner. He'll always get my
nod. He could probably play for Arsenal, Real Madrid - or
Manchester United too, But Christophe. You'll never be as
adored, than by us Brummies that worship you.

The ones that got away

PART ONE: Graham Taylor (Resigned)

WHEN GRAHAM TAYLOR first marched into Villa Park in May 1987, he took one look at his new "home" and immediately declared, "this place is a shambles". He was right. Taylor had left the secure surroundings of Watford's Vicarage Road to tackle the mounting carnage of Villa Park. Within three years he had steered the club out of second division obscurity and guided them to a runners-up spot in division one. The achievement won him the England manager's job.

Football's long and winding road, however, has a nasty habit of turning full circle. Taylor returned to manage Villa in February 2002. After just 15 months in the hot seat he discovered the harsh truth - the club was still a shambles.

He left three days after the end of the season. But this wasn't a decision based on bad results. It went much deeper than that. There were no raised voices, no argument. Taylor hadn't got the heart for a bitter dogfight at this stage of his career, and anyway, he was better than that. Instead, he simply turned his back on what had become an impossible situation. He admitted defeat against the two men who were running the club in a way that he just couldn't swallow. He clashed with Doug Ellis, the chairman, and in particular, Mark Ansell, the club's financial director, boardroom powerbroker - and Doug's 'deadlier-than-thou' sidekick. It was the end of the road.

On Saturday, March 22, *Brum's the Word* announced the arrival of a new group of Villa fans committed to bringing about sweeping change throughout the club - from top to bottom. Professor Carl Chinn, their spokesman, said: "The club is in terminal decline. It's time for Doug Ellis to take a long, hard look at himself. He must accept responsibility for the unrest and think seriously. If he doesn't have the money, or the inclination to move Villa forward, he should stand aside."

On Wednesday, May 14, Taylor, just hours after his resignation, said: "The structure of the club has to be looked at on and off the field. People have to be able to look at themselves and say it's time for change. Contrary to what may be perceived, playing results are not the reason for my resignation."

On Friday, May 16, Villa's European Cup-winning captain Dennis Mortimer weighed in. "I'm lending my name to the campaign for change at the top," he said. "With the current board in place, any new manager simply hasn't got a chance."

It seems that everyone is singing from the same hymn sheet - except for the Villa Park Two. The supporters have a new manager, but the cynical among them reckon that Ellis and Ansell have simply re-arranged the deck chairs on The Titanic.

Meanwhile, Graham Taylor OBE, remained noble in his resignation. As he cleared out his drawers, he must have looked back on an eventful past, and pondered a future without the unwanted 'extra pressures' of the game. He may never step into a football manager's office again. He will be sorely missed.

Worksop's most famous son had been a manager for more than 30 years. He was put in charge of Lincoln City in 1972 after his playing career was cut short by a hip injury. In 1977 he was wanted by West Bromwich Albion to take over at The Hawthorns from Johnny Giles, but Taylor was unimpressed by the Albion board during his interview and on a whim, joined Elton John's Watford. He famously took the Hornets from the fourth division to the first division in five seasons.

His biggest challenge, and greatest honour, was managing England, even though he was vilified in the papers for his long-ball tactics and was cruelly labelled "Turnip head". He was also mocked following his "Do I not like that" line in a television documentary chronicling England's failure to reach the World Cup finals in 1994.

But despite the barrage of abuse, he has remained one of the most respected and likeable figures in the game.

Of course, in his second spell at Villa, things didn't go well on the field. The club finished just three points above the relegation zone, managing one league win away from home. Two defeats against arch rivals Birmingham City forced Taylor to the brink. He famously walked away from a live television interview after the derby game at Villa Park too furious to trust himself to speak to the nation. To rub salt into the already gaping wounds, Blues finished three places higher in the Premiership table.

With his club starring relegation in the face, Taylor admitted that he was finding the situation off the field, hard to take. "This has been a difficult season and I have spent far too much time dealing with private agendas off the pitch to know exactly where the club is going," he said. "It has been hard work and you do sometimes ask yourself what it's all about."

Almost before the last ball had been kicked, Dion Dublin, the Ballet lover, was quick to put the boot in. He described Villa's season as both rubbish and embarrassing. Neither he nor the rest of the squad were at Villa Park on the day that Graham Taylor turned his back on the club for good. They were enjoying a drink at a retirement party for Jim Paul, Villa's long-serving kit man. News filtered through the function room by word of mouth. Many were shocked. Nearly all were dismayed.

When they arrived for the retirement do, which took place at a local pub, the players were given a glass of champagne to raise for the man who had loyally washed the club's claret and blue shirts for 27 years. The toast was, "a long and happy retirement". They didn't realise that, just down the road, their manager was planning a long and happy retirement of his own.

Taylor, still defiantly wearing his trademark boyish grin, said: "I resigned from Aston Villa because I disagreed with how the club was being run. Now, I need to have some fun in my life."

It's the very least he deserves.

The ones that got away

PART TWO: West Bromwich Albion (relegated)

PIGS WEARING LIPSTICK. That's how West Bromwich Albion were cruelly labelled as they took their first tentative steps into the promised land after 16 years in the football wilderness.

Experts were convinced the writing was on the wall before a ball had been kicked. Bookmakers offered 2-7 on the drop, making Albion the shortest priced favourites for relegation since the Premiership began. But Gary Megson, the manager who had "achieved the impossible" by hauling his team back into the big time, valiantly shrugged off the merchants of doom. He urged his players to react like top class golfers. "The ones that are successful are those who hole the putts," he reasoned.

And so, Albion took their Premiership bow at Old Trafford's Theatre of Dreams. The prospect was mouth watering for the long suffering fans. Starved of glory for a decade and a half, they now proudly stood shoulder to shoulder with Europe's finest. Some gazed around the stadium in awe, determined to drink in every last second of what was a glittering occasion. For the youngsters in the crowd, this was dreamland - a first taste of paradise. To others it was a flashback to the days of Jeff Astle, Tony 'Bomber' Brown and Cyrille Regis.

For a while, the fantasy continued. In September, three wins in a row put Albion above Manchester United in the league and the supporters were setting their sights on Europe. The pigs were preparing to fly.

Megson was flying too. His popularity in the Black Country soared to such an extent that he was made Lord of the Manor of West Bromwich. On his inauguration night, a misty November evening at Birmingham's Botanical Gardens, he shuffled nervously into the banqueting hall flanked by two wandering minstrels. Before him a pair of cackling serving wenches were thrown unceremoniously into the stocks by way of a sacrifice. Unfortunately for screaming Lord Megson, the medieval tomfoolery marked the beginning of the end of his wonderful Premiership adventure.

"The Premier League is bent - one penalty all season and the referees against us every game. That's the price you pay for being an unfashionable club," wailed the Baggies diehards as the team began to fade hopelessly away. Their frustrations were somewhat born out when Megson sent a "video nasty" to Philip Don, the referees' supervisor, highlighting a number of "questionable decisions" against his team. Don called the game's 24 elite officials together for an emergency briefing - nothing seemed to change.

The transfer window was Albion's last hope. The "pigs" needed to go to market - but they refused to spend a penny. It was a crushing blow to the supporters who were now forced to buckle down for an impossible relegation battle. In a way the club had sealed its own fate. "If we go bankrupt the fans won't have a team to support at all," the management argued. "You've blown our big opportunity - you haven't even given us a chance," the downhearted faithful replied.

Even the previously untouchable Megson was coming in for criticism. His stubborn reluctance to play Black Country folk hero Bob Taylor in his testimonial year was aggravating supporters. By the middle of March, the manager had resigned himself to relegation. "We're up the creek," he said after a 2-0 home defeat against Chelsea. The final nail in the coffin came at Birmingham City. Geoff Horsfield's winning goal four minutes into injury time summed up Albion's luckless season. It was the end of the road - and everyone in the ground knew it. The players left St Andrew's dejected. Many of the fans were reduced to tears.

Still, though, they kept their enthusiasm and sense of humour - and they steadfastly refused to stop boinging. At Blackburn, as a "mark of respect" to Premiership officials, nearly all of the 4,000 travelling spectators dressed as referees (except for one who attended the game as a giraffe). "At least this should get us recognised," said one supporter. "The definition of a Baggie?" he asked. "You have to wait until after midnight to catch a glimpse of your team on *Match of the Day*."

Albion received only one thrashing all season, a 6-0 drubbing by Liverpool at The Hawthorns - the worst home defeat in the club's history. But for all the near misses and debatable decisions, the team - with the exception of Russell Hoult and Jason Koumas - had nowhere near enough quality to compete at the highest level. Lee Hughes, on his return from Coventry City, was disappointing and Jason Roberts, billed by some as a possible successor to his uncle Cyrille Regis as the "new messiah", scored just three goals.

On the last day of the season, with the team long since doomed, the paying customers again took centre stage. They were serenaded by their Newcastle counterparts who couldn't resist a few bars of the Dame Vera Lynn classic *We'll meet again*. At the final whistle, both sets of supporters gave each other a standing ovation. One heavily tattooed man screamed "I love you" as he applauded the Baggies on their "lap of honour".

A flabby gent, dressed horribly wrong for the occasion in an ill-fitting, stained grey jacket that barely covered his magnolia and pink cheesecloth shirt, kissed a small "West Bromwich Albion FA Cup winners 1968" metal badge that was pinned awkwardly to his breast pocket.

BRUM'S THE WORD

Sweating like a glassblower's backside, he turned to his fellow fans. You could tell by his face that he'd got a point to make. "I'd watch this team in any division," he said, barely able to hold back the tears. "I'd follow them out of the league and back again. It's in here, you see," he added thumping his chest. "Anyone who is gutted that we're out of the Premiership was only ever here for the glamour in the first place."